Something  Under the
Sun

MW01096928

SOMETHING NEW UNDER THE SUN

The History of America's First Car

Carol Jean Lambert

great-granddaughter
of
John W. Lambert
Inventor of America's gasoline-powered automobile
1891

Copyright @ Carol Jean Lambert Clinton, MA 2012

www.caroljeanlambertbooks.com

ISBN: 978-1-939166-31-9 (paperback)
ISBN: 978-1-939166-32-6 (ebook)

Library of Congress Control Number: 2013956709

All rights reserved. No part of this book may be reproduced in any form or by any electronic or mechanical means, including information storage and retrieval systems, without permission in writing from the publisher, except by a reviewer who may quote brief passages in a review.

Merrimack Media, Cambridge, Massachusetts

Contents

Introduction

I became a fan of my great-grandfather John Lambert simply by being born. The love and admiration I have now lay quiet for fifty some years. Occasionally the gleam of pride in his historical accomplishment would rise to my mind but did not blossom full-blown until one particular trip back to Ohio. My Dad had taken my son and me on a family history tour in 2000 to Anderson, Indiana, Greenville and Union City, Ohio which of course included talk about his grandfather John Lambert who was an automotive pioneer and who had been established by *Antique Automobile*, the official publication of the Antique Automobile Club of America, as the builder of the first car to run by gasoline in America. Although we didn't drive all the way up to Ohio City, Ohio, that is where he made his horseless carriage and drove it in January 1891. As Dad talked I saw in my mind's eye a pen in my hand and under it, a stack of pages filled with writing. I decided I would write about my great-grandfather and his mammoth but largely unknown achievement of designing, building and driving America's first gasoline-powered car. Everyone knows who the Wright Brothers are; is not the car as important as the airplane? I would tell the world about the inventor of America's gasoline automobile. He was one of the first in America to champion a gasoline-powered engine and became famous for his unique designs. He became a rich man selling engines before his gasoline-fueled cars ever sold. Fifteen years of successful production of Lambert-designed automobiles did not begin until 1902.

I came home from my trip with Dad to spend hours on the Internet where I found dozens of interesting websites packed full of automotive facts and leads to other websites and sources to write for more information from helpful historical institutions. This mad casting of my research nets lasted several years. I traveled to the Midwest to visit libraries and interview those few left who knew him. I kept up a conversation with my elderly Dad who called John *"Grandfather"* and who until recently owned the two antique Lambert cars I grew up with, beautiful vehicles with shiny brass lamps and leather seats, and I asked other family members about their own file drawers of John Lambert information. I got to spend hours with John's granddaughter-in-law from Anderson who knew John's wife Minnie as well and who helped care for them both in their later years. A kind and sensitive woman, she was present when John died. She and her daughter graciously let me sit for five days at their dining room table (not once, but twice) going through a large trunk of John Lambert's papers and family photographs, allowing me to copy at will. I traveled to Ohio and visited libraries and old homesteads. I wrote to dozens of libraries, museums and automotive clubs scattered across the Midwest including the rich resources of the renowned National Automotive History Collection at the Detroit Public Library and the Henry Ford Museum. In Indiana I toured John's house and spent a spellbinding afternoon with Anderson historians Dan and Barb Davis who have collected John Lambert memorabilia for a lifetime. Among their collection of brochures and pictures, papers and hubcaps, they have a miniature re-creation of the first car and all the pieces of a 1912 Lambert touring vehicle out in the barn. On a return trip I had the rare opportunity to watch them run their prized Lambert gasoline engine, one of very few known to exist that were manufactured before the car days. I danced to the syncopation on the green clover of their backyard, thinking, *John heard this sound.*

I had reams of information to organize and ponder concerning antique engines and cars, Ohio history and early natural gas strikes in Indiana and the rise of the automobile industry there. I read about the Civil War, the Industrial Revolution, Thomas Edison and Mark Twain, about Ransom Olds and Henry Ford, Charles and Frank Duryea, Elwood Haynes and the Wright Brothers. I had my own file of old family papers, merely copies of earlier written material that provided a structure on which to hang my story. There is the handwritten family tree that goes back to John's grandparents Mike and Betsy from Lost Mountain, Pennsylvania and the letter written by John's older sister Libby that describes their early childhood on a farm in Champaign County, Ohio near or perhaps indeed at John's birthplace. There is the collection of documents Ray, John's son and my grandfather, collected in his effort to win recognition for his father's car: a four-page list of pertinent questions answered in John's own hand about his early automotive experiences, a four-page single-spaced essay Ray wrote of his own memories and his collection of affidavits from witnesses to that first car. There have been references in family talk of a briefcase misplaced or stolen, back between the two World Wars, holding papers and affidavits with signatures from the men of that moment, acknowledging John's prototype as the first successful attempt of all of them to build America's first gasoline car but that is only a thought in the air now. In spite of what Ray may have lost, he did succeed in certifying what his father had done by preserving the original photograph and collecting certified statements from actual witnesses. In October/November 1960, in order to declare once and for all who was first, after five full years of extensive investigation and research, L. Scott Bailey, the Editor of *Antique Automobile* magazine and Editor of the definitive and beautiful book *The American Car Since 1775*, elucidated the claim that John Lambert built the first car to run by gasoline in America in an article entitled, "Historic Discovery: 1891 Lambert, New Claim for America's First Car." *Antique Automobile* is the official publication of the Antique Automobile Club of America, America's oldest automobile historical society. In correspondence, Mr. Bailey encouraged me in my quest to tell John's story. In my research, I located various clippings from newspapers, county and town histories with references to John Lambert. Very exciting was the discovery of articles and pictures in old magazines and encyclopedias, each a delicious piece of my sumptuous story. I am lucky to benefit from the work of L. Scott Bailey and Dan Davis, both automobile historians who took a special interest in my great grandfather.

The more I learned the more I understood how much more there is to learn. I became and still am a devoted student of my subject. I wrote a novel about those early Lamberts and feel as though I know them.

John operated from within a large family dynasty. He may have started as a poor farm boy but by the time he reached his full height of 6'2" his father was a successful manufacturer in the Industrial Age and John had proved his inventive genius with his nationwide sellers of farm tool innovations. The family could hardly have been more favorably situated for an inventive young mechanic to explore his love of engines and his dream of a self-propelled car.

Chapter 1

The Corn Planter

Not every family has a genius in it. I didn't know this as a little girl because I took so much for granted. Without question I willingly climbed onto the sideboard of my father's antique car, a 1910 Lambert touring wagon, between the two thick-spoked wooden wheels, stepped up through the little leather-covered U-shaped door and held on to the shiny brass handle to position myself on the puckered upholstered bench seat. I had no idea what the car represented. In this scene of the past I was perhaps nine or ten years old. My father had bought this car, built by his grandfather, in 1956 in its original condition, not restored, but well preserved and running. What a find! And did he love it! I thought all fathers had a special toy with which to entertain the family. All four kids could fit into the backseat; the two boys jockeyed for space on either edge. Mom and the family dog sat up front. I followed my sister who happily sat in the center. Dad checked several items around the car and asked us to admire the shine of the polished brass before he pulled on the glass windshield to unfold it in order to double the protection against on-coming insects and wind. Looking back I realize he probably spent hours preparing for an outing. All parts were shiny and running at once, an orchestration done by Dad. Because Dad didn't work on the engine himself he relied on mechanics who out of their passion for old engines kept this antique running. These things I surmised later on. Daughters were not included in the behind-the-scenes operations and responsibilities but were certainly expected to join in the display and enjoyment. The top to the vehicle was folded flat behind us out of the way. Ours was an open-air ride.

The car started by means of a crank that was attached to the front face of the car. With a battery providing juice, Dad did the cranking. It was a difficult and dangerous task. All of our attention was on him. With the rest of us in position on our seats, he paused hunched in front of the car while the crank handle rested in his fingers. With each effort, I could see him give a twist of his shoulder with a great heave. The exertion exhilarated him; he cranked the car while directing us kids to sit down and hold on. When the engine kicked in and the noise began, he rushed to a lever by the steering wheel to adjust the choke and advance the spark. As soon as the car caught, it became animated. It was a tense moment for me to see no one behind the steering wheel and the car suddenly alive. His dash to the driver's seat was awesome. I imagined us taking off driverless but Dad always hopped aboard. Sliding behind the wheel, he then managed to accelerate and honk the horn at the same time. With Mom and our exuberant pet beside him up front and the four of us kids in the rear seat, he took us out for a ride. We rode on the wide shaded streets of my Dayton, Ohio neighborhood, passed manicured lawns sprawling in front of large Georgian style mansions. With my father at the wheel, I never thought to consider how unusual it was to be out riding in a car that was half a century old. Only once or twice throughout that childhood did I hear about John Lambert, and not as "the genius in our family" but rather as Daddy's "Grandfather". Back then I did not understand the prodigious significance of John Lambert's career or the unique achievement that was linked to the loud and intoxicating rides in the old Lambert car.

The car went amazingly far; we puttered around the back-country roads and passed through intersections of main streets with traffic lights and modern cars all about. Dad was not shy about being on the road. He honked and gave commentary as he drove. A lively guy anyway, my Dad sparked as much as the car. He took us a considerable way into parts that had significant challenges, especially the section called Hills and Dales. The road was narrow with sharp up and down inclines that we took at what seemed like top speed, possibly 25 mph. In fact the car could achieve 60 mph. Dad says now he often took it out onto the highway but never with me. With warnings to look out for low tree branches, we seemed to be the only ones going through the woods down by Houk Stream. Then back into civilization we became the sight to see as neighbors waved from their verandas. I suppose the old folks on those verandas remembered when horses ruled the road and the few gas-powered machines they may have seen back then looked an awful lot like our Lambert. Even as a little girl I knew my Dad, part showman, part salesman, loved this exhibition.

The two cubical brass kerosene lanterns sitting on each side of the windshield fascinated me. The headlights were out in front of the car like the cars I was used to but the lanterns were an anomaly. I never saw any of them lighted. Dad said these cars had not been made to go out after dark so the lights were mostly for show. They were polished perfectly with labor done by my brothers. Earlier in the afternoon I had peeked through the second story window above the driveway of our house and overheard their groans as Dad commanded more elbow grease. Before the ride, they competed to squeeze the big rubber balloon of the horn attached to its spot near the driver on the right-hand side of the car, but Dad on the road saved this task for himself. Honk! Honk! The original horn had a sound all its own. We went to the street where my grandmother lived, the horn honking like a goose and she came outside smiling to wave at our passing. Dad knew she would not step inside the old car and that its sight brought mixed emotions.

Theirs was a strong connection. She was a softhearted woman and missed the old days of glory the car represented. We all knew she was sad about losing her husband Ray whose father had been The Genius. To her, John Lambert the car builder had been a kind-hearted and generous father-in-law who had lived to a ripe old age. Both men were gone within a couple of years of each other and we children had hardly a direct memory of either man among us.

Laughing in pleasure at the sight of his mother, Dad stopped the vehicle and hopped down to check the engine fluid levels and perhaps add a little oil while she doled out kisses to us grandchildren over the rattle of the car, which shook with the hard-working engine. The noise of the car precluded conversation. My Dad and grandmother had firsthand knowledge of the automobile business John Lambert helped create. The shadow of the man was as real as the blue smoke gathering as the car idled. Mother and son had no need to tell each other what they both knew to be true. Out of consideration for my mother who probably tired of talk of The Genius long before any of us kids were born, the two original Lamberts never did talk in the family group – or to me – about their mutual pride in their Lambert legacy. Their memories went unspoken about what John had done, the cars he designed and the company of automotive giants he kept, the Dodge Brothers, The Chevrolet boys, Ransom Olds. I never heard them talk about the pre-World War One family enterprise that produced three thousand automobiles for sale in a year and employed hundreds of people. As a small girl, I never heard firsthand accounts of John's gentleness and ready laugh, or his constant need to apply his ideas to the mechanical world. It was not until my own middle age that I began to ask questions and to research the life of the man who, born into a world of horse-driven wooden buggies and simple stationary steam-powered machines, concentrated his inventive intellect on pioneering the automobile, more specifically the gasoline engine and his own unique system of transmission. With a peck to his mother's cheek and with all fluid levels checked, Dad was back in the driver's seat and we motored back home. Dad pulled the car into the middle garage. Second in enthusiasm for riding in the old car was Cinnamon the family dog. She remained in her spot by the driver's pedals long after the engine was quiet and the other six of us had gone into the house, just in case Dad would turn around and take the car out for another spin.

John William Lambert was born in 1860, a year before the Civil War began. At that time births were not yet officially recorded in Ohio and any physical evidence there may have been of the event has since been lost. John's arrival, however, put a process in motion that has passed through his son and grandson to me, his great-granddaughter as well as to all twelve great-grandchildren. Because of this vibrant legacy, as I researched I found grand-nieces and nephews who knew of him as well. One niece proudly shared a photograph of her grandfather, John's brother-in-law, in a Lambert car.

Family records show John's birth as happening in Champaign County, Ohio, near Mechanicsburg on a Sunday morning after a heavy snowfall January 29, 1860. According to what was usual in those times he was likely born at home in his family's farmhouse, for his Pennsylvania-born father was a farmer. There would have been no electricity or running water. The floors were most likely packed dirt or wood. The winter's cold was kept at bay by fires in the hearth. John was the third child of George and Anna Lambert, who had arrived as a young couple from the mountains of Pennsylvania to farmland near Springfield, Ohio. They thrived and had ten children altogether. Although new to Ohio, the Lamberts had family nearby; there is evidence that one and possibly all three of George's older brothers also moved from the mountains of Pennsylvania to live in Ohio with their families. One brother later returned to Harrisburg but left his children in Ohio. These cousins became a part of George and Anna's household. John's mother, Christiana (nee Lieber), had a mother, stepfather and half-brother in Ohio as well. According to family records, her grandfather was a wealthy baker in New York. George, her husband and my great-great-grandfather, was a farmer and livestock operator who later became a manufacturer of carriage parts. As people in their situation commonly did, it is likely my great-great-grandparents walked from Lost Mountain, PA to central Ohio beside oxen pulling a wooden cart of belongings.

Ohio's natural resources were great for the early farmers. There was regular rainfall and plenty of sunshine. It was only a few dozen years prior, a speck in evolutionary time, that the area was covered with primeval hardwood forests, mulching the forest floor for eons so that the soil was abundantly rich for the pioneers who cleared the land of those trees to farm their crops. Many Ohio farmers of George's era did very well financially by supplying Mr. Lincoln's army with food to eat and leather to wear. All signs indicate George was one of them. Ohio was far from the fighting and the war provided a robust market for all northern farmers. John lived in the midst of the family's success. He was part of a large sibling group and even larger extended family. The world of his young childhood, although shadowed by the fear and atrocities of four long years of Civil War, was likely relatively secure and healthy. In his time, children were expected to contribute significantly to the work on the farm. Children routinely helped with planting, carrying water to the workers in the sun, weeding, tending animals and many other of the endless often repetitive tasks on a prosperous farm. With all that physical activity and fresh air, John grew up physically strong and hard working. I bet little JW spent much of his time working outside and that it did not take him long to distinguish himself as talented with tools and machines.

Shortly after the Civil War ended, George moved his family to the western edge of Ohio, to Darke County, named after General William Darke, a Revolutionary War hero. George bought land near historic Greenville where Mad Anthony Wayne signed the Peace Treaty with the Indians, to a town that was little more than a cross in the roads, called Hill Grove. Today it is not much bigger and the spelling has become Hillgrove. There is a beautiful red brick home with two-story pillars on the site now and likely was the home George lived in with his growing family. It shows a comfortable grandeur and indicates the adjustment the teenaged John was called on to make with this move across state as his farmer father also became a manufacturer. George was expanding his horizons and taking on the challenges and rewards of producing tools and parts for buggies and farm wagons. The family had a new home and new routines, in a new community with new people to get to know. A railroad line crossed a corner of the property and connected George to the manufacturing facilities he built in nearby Union, now called Union City, a village where originally five railroad lines came together. John's father was hereafter involved in some way in the manufacture of wagons and carriages, so it was not a huge jump for John to spend his time imagining improvements to horse-drawn transportation.

In order to understand the significance of what I was learning as I gathered patent information on my great-grandfather, I reconstructed in more detail my knowledge of American agricultural history and (with the help of Hollywood and American artists) drew pictures in my mind of what farm life was like in John's era. At the time of the Civil War, farming methods were mostly all manual and consequently labor intensive. The work was dirty and very slow. As a farm boy himself, John had intimate knowledge of just how true this was. In order to produce a row of corn a farmer (or perhaps a farmer's son) first had to plow the dirt, embed and then cover hand-counted kernels of seed. This took a very long time and was backbreaking work. In only a generation there would be horse-powered machines that planted multiple rows of corn all at once. In the meantime, innovative American farmers applied their creativity to devising laborsaving machines, many of which were useful but none so much as a simple little corn planter that for its time revolutionized tedious fieldwork. John was of prime age to lend his muscle power to jobs that needed to be done on his father's farm in this post Civil War era. He was at the very heart of the "laboratory" and he stepped to the very forefront of the mechanical revolution. In the mid-1870's as a fifteen-year-old he came up with an idea to improve the farmers' lot of the planting season. He built a handheld wooden devise that dug the hole and deposited a specific number of the kernels into the ground, all in one gesture. It was a clever little machine that looks now like a hospital crutch. In its time it greatly reduced necessary planting time and freed farmers to do other tasks or plant larger fields. A farmer could plant a row of corn in one-tenth the time as before. Word of John's devise must have spread quickly. It was not long before the Lamberts were selling them nationwide.

The patent for the corn-planter is only one page long and needed less than two months to be granted. Peculiar though it may be, John's father made the application and signs the patent description as though the invention were his and not that of his sixteen-year-old son. Patent No. 178,166 is dated May 30, 1876. The signature of George Lambert appears as "Inventor" along with those of two witnesses and an attorney. This was probably done for legal reasons and at no time later did George dispute crediting his son. John is credited in several places including his obituary. In the patent, the corn-planter is described as "simple, cheap and durable and not liable to get out of order." Oh, how I wish I could see one of those little wonders today! Please, check your barns and sheds. Could one still be hiding out somewhere? One of my brothers recently acquired for me another tool built by the Lambert Brothers. This tool was manufactured in 1888 in the same plant in Union City in which the corn-planters were produced a dozen years prior. It is a beam auger. A tool for farmers used to build their barns, it has a heavy metal eight-inch long screw which is turned by two opposing handles enhanced by three metal-teeth gears. It will bore a hole in a wooden barn beam so the beams can be pegged together. It is a drill of oak and metal construction with brackets to hold the beam end in place and is about twice the size of a thigh master (and the same shape). The mechanisms of John's corn planter are described in the patent in concise, practical terms so that I believe I know how it worked. The way the kernels were counted, held back and then released resembles the trick of a "Chinese bank", a little slide toy found in joke shops. In one motion of the one arm, the readied kernels travel down a tube as the ground hole is made and receives the seeds. At the same time the next set of kernels is readied for the next thrust.

One year prior to the patent for the corn planter is a patent for another John Lambert invention, a hay-rake and loader. This was a devise to be attached behind a wagon pulled by a horse. I find these old machines especially beautiful. The forward motion of the horse got the cut and binder mechanisms going. A little mechanical escalator was put into motion at the same time which brought the hay to the wagon. The end result was a cleared field and a wagon filled with bundles of hay. Imagine pulling a wagon through your back yard that dragged a two-wheeled devise with blades to cut grass and metal-fingered "hands" to scoop the cut grass up into your wagon. John's device combined these tasks to save time. The farmer needing to cut and gather his hay could do it in one sweep of his field. Prior to the machines, they would cut and bind by hand and then collect the bundles while walking beside a horse-pulled wagon. It was a physical job and many farmers were rightly proud of their speed and technique. Different farmers used different binding knots, providing grist for discussions in the off-season about whose knot was better and for competitions at Fair time. The modest distribution of the Lambert hay rake and loader was a prelude to the wide commercial success of their corn planter.

When the patent protection for the corn planter arrived, George Lambert was ready for his son's Big Hit. Like many entrepreneurs of his day, George was constantly on the look out for items to manufacture that would sell in the marketplace. He developed his plant in Union along very practical lines. Being a farmer himself of many years, he knew what farmers wanted to buy so that is what he produced. Wooden wagon parts were constantly needed to replace pieces of the main work vehicle of the farm. Except for the horse, the common wagon and the less common carriage were the main methods of transport. George established a successful enterprise. He built his clientele and distribution systems; he established a group of workers, men and boys loyal to his outfit and willing to learn the new methods needed to produce the ever-changing Lambert product line. He developed his feel for marketing and plant management while John developed his ideas for new tools for the field and improvements to what existed. Perhaps a major motivation for George to go into manufacturing was John's inventiveness. This father-teenage son team, with John's older brother Al involved in the business end, created an agricultural sensation. Reports from back then describe the Lambert corn planter as a popular tool for busy farmers planting fields across the nation. I can imagine competitions organized to test the speed of the planter against other corn planters, community events that maybe pit neighboring farms against farmers from another county. In my imagination John's devise always won.

One of the most thrilling pieces of Lambert memorabilia I was able to lay my hands on is a hand-written letter from George to his son John. I found it in the trunk of Lambert things in Florida. Dated in the momentous year of 1891, the letter is remarkable to me. The day and month of its date are my son's birthday and the beautiful letterhead is decorated with one of my personal symbols. The four-leaf clovers intertwined with the names Lambert-Parent & Co. could have been designed for me. I can spot a four-leaf clover as I walk along, a talent my grandfather Ray also had. Clover appears on the letterhead no doubt because it is a good friend to farmers who rotate their fields with a year of red clover to replenish the soil. The letter itself is an example of how the Lambert men worked together. The content of the letter is a father reporting and advising his son.

The A neckyoaks (yokes) whe (we) can't get them out fast anouth (enough) and are you doing iny (any) thing on the ingen (engine) (?) Concerning the paten (patent) on the chair thare (there) is someny (so many) out that I don't suppose that thare (there) half of them patent (patented)(.) And the wone (one) that sels (sells) the most is the one that makes the money (.) the (The) people won't try to make one like another(.) Torfere (therefore) tha (they) will get in trouble. And I would think that whe (we) can make as much with it as if it was patened (patented).

It reads like John had an innovation for a "chair" (probably a car/buggy seat, possibly from this first automobile prototype) that his father thought did not need patent protection. "Don't wait for the patent, just sell them!" the father tells the son. "The one who sells the most makes the most money." He reasons to his son that the copycats will not copy John's chair exactly anyway to avoid getting in trouble. I'm fascinated that he asks John about his work on the engine by which I assume he is referring to the stationery version of the gasoline model John had built and used to propel his horseless carriage of that year. This is probably why this particular letter survived all this time. Certainly the letter is further evidence of John's car having been completed early in 1891. By April, the date of the letter, having received no orders for the automobile, the Lamberts' interest had turned to John's new version of the engine. The father signs the letter "Yours truly, G.Lambert".

George could not have had any formal education. Prussian immigrants such as George's parents had a reputation for educational fervor, so that it's fair for me to imagine George learning his ABC's at home with his three older brothers and four younger sisters in their Pennsylvania mountain home. He was certainly literate. His cursive handwriting is steady and even and shows confidence. His spelling is phonetic. I loved figuring out "ingen" to be "engine". And "torfere" to be "therefore". I look at old photos of George and I can hear his voice, "ingen," "torfere." In this letter to his son John, George is directive, respectful and smart.

This is the history I found of the highly successful family pattern of using John's ideas for their product line. John's wooden mechanical corn planting device received a lot of attention and was heralded and imitated. The success of the corn-planter must have been tremendous encouragement to the imagination of this young man. He saw his idea bring added wealth to his family and bring relief not only to himself as he labored in the field, but also to farmers everywhere. It was a major contribution to agricultural productivity.

Chapter 2

Ohio City Success

The time came in the 1870's when the generous land of the nation's Midwest offered up oil and natural gas. Gas strikes were being made from Pennsylvania to Illinois that provided an abundant and cheap source of fuel. Ohioans tapped it to help create a frenzy of manufacturing growth. George was not alone in his entrepreneurship. A saying of the time tells the story: "Like men sought gold in California a generation ago, now men seek inventions in Ohio." It was the Industrial Revolution. Tinkering was a popular hobby and became the source for many products. Eager businessmen scoured the nook and cranny workshops throughout the countryside to find salable items. Ohio was exploding with new products and new means of production and transportation. Soon it would have more patents per capita than any other state in the Union. Railroads were being built to connect small towns everywhere. Not only were inventors coming up with better ways to do just about everything, but also entrepreneurs were developing new configurations for assembling their products using new tools and equipment. By this time Ohio inventors had contributed such widely used conveniences and big hits for the entrepreneurs as the stepladder, barbed wire and the flat-bottomed grocery bag. Commercial chewing gum and Ivory soap were also conceived and manufactured in Ohio at this time. Bustling with expectation for new ideas, the public was fascinated with gadgets and clamored for more. The market for tools and machines that made life easier and more productive seemed insatiable. The challenge was to get the product and the manufacturer together, to hook up the workshops and the inventors with the factories and the business people. The Lamberts had their inventor and their business organization all within the family.

Over the years, John and his five brothers stepped in turn into the family business started by their father. Brothers-in-law were involved, too. The Lamberts were a large, energetic, clever family who were blessed with good health, strong minds and the ability to see and seize opportunity. It was a marvelous situation for a maturing mechanical genius to discover and exercise his talents. Encouraged by his family and the success of his ideas, encouraged by a market hungry for new and improved devices, John could dream grandiose dreams.

My brothers and sister may agree with me that growing up among the four of us seemed like a lot of siblings. Consequently I can only try to imagine John's experience with so many more. It took me some time to research and get to know John's birth family of four girls and six boys but I felt it was incumbent upon me to learn their stories as individuals in order to properly get to know my great-grandfather. What I found touched me as in my mind they took life.

John's oldest sibling was a sister, Elizabeth, called Libby. She married Dan Cook when she was just sixteen. If her parents were disappointed by her tender young age at her marriage, they were able to put it aside in order to welcome her husband into their family. Libby's choice had much in common with the enterprising Lamberts in his association with the Pioneer Pole and Shaft Company, which ever after had a long history intertwined with the Lambert companies. The Cooks were involved in this company located in a town 20-30 miles from Union, close enough to be compatible, far enough to avoid competition. Over the years, there were many advantageous reciprocal arrangements between the two companies.

The oldest male child, George Albert, who often signed his name GA Lambert, was referred to as "Al" in family papers. As the oldest son, Al was first to join their father in the business; at various times he appears on the letterhead as President, Treasurer, etc. He was described as the moneyman. He married Eva Parent from a premiere family who were among the co-founders of Jackson Township in Darke County. Eva's father inherited and ran the lucrative Parent Granary in Union, an enterprise in which Al participated periodically. When my great-grandfather, the Lambert's second-born son came of age, his name shows up on paper as part of the Lambert family enterprise and he calls himself JW as well as John. These two oldest brothers shouldered much of the leadership responsibilities for the Lambert companies in the years to come. From what I understand they were very different in personality and in looks. Family photographs show their physical contrasts; Al looked more like their father with his slight frame and handsome long face; JW favored his mother with her round, soft-featured face and her tall hearty build. Their individual skills complimented each other, John being visionary and inventive, Al being a money manager and sales expert.

John's next younger sibling was a sister, but they lost her as a young toddler when John was only three. We know she was remembered and revered, because when John moved his elderly parents to Indiana in the 1890's, her grave was moved from its location on the Urbana farm in Champaign County to the cemetery in Anderson. After this poor little girl, George and Anna had six additional healthy children, two girls and four boys. I have read so much about John's parents George and Christiana ("Anna") I feel on some level I know them. On a trip to Anderson I sought out their graves and when I found the three identical stones, for George, Christiana and eight-month-old Savina, I burst into tears. I stood there and cried (Flood of 2004) for people I had never met yet who are parts of me. A side note involves the

Great Easter Flood of 1913, an actual devastating act of nature in the Midwest that converted parts of six states into a frigid inland sea. The torrential rains (parts of Ohio received eleven inches) expelled the old Lambert coffins from their underground resting places in the sloping banks of the Anderson River. When the water receded, John arranged to have them re-interred in higher ground near other family members at the site I visited. There is a large Lambert memorial stone at this prominent location in Maplewood Cemetery and around it are the remains of many Lamberts and Lambert relatives. John's nephew, Al's only son Homer, ran the West Maplewood Cemetery for many years. During the 1913 Flood, which put hundreds of thousands of people across the Midwest in dire peril, the Lamberts managed to get an engine to the Anderson *Herald*, so that important information could be distributed in spite of the power outage.

Emma was the child born after Savina and appears to have had a special closeness with my great-grandfather. As a young woman she married an older widower with a small child. After having two additional children they apparently separated. Although there was no divorce she lived in Anderson near her brother while her husband (named, I'm not kidding – Isaac Newton Glunt) remained in Greenville. At the end of his life he was buried by the KKK. Can't imagine why Emma couldn't get along with him. After Emma was a brother Christian Harry. As well as participating in the family business he had several successful automobile-related enterprises of his own. Then came Mollie. She and Emma appear to have been very close. Mollie married Harvey Longnecker, an old neighbor who kept the books for the Lamberts for many years, but both died relatively young. Emma lived a long life. She attended John's funeral in 1952 and died the following year.

The last three children were all boys. Did I mention how healthy their mother Anna looks in the one photo I have of her? She had to have been a hearty woman to survive so many children and the strenuous demands of the farm. The seventh child, and fourth boy, was named after a hero of George and Christiana's generation and was no doubt meant as a salute to their Pennsylvania roots. I get such a kick out of the old names. Benjamin Franklin Lambert was born in 1868 and called "Frank"; he was often in the family business and served as President of the engine-producing Buckeye Manufacturing Company for a number of years while John ran the car business. There was a four-year gap before Samuel "Sam" Webster arrived and, then, almost three years later during which time they became grandparents, George and Anna welcomed the final baby, Levi Calvin whom they called "Babe". In adulthood he was "Cal". These last two children had a different childhood experience than their older siblings and did not settle in Anderson or Greenville as adults like the others, but moved on to St. Petersburg, Florida looking, the stories say, for profits in the land boom going on there at the time.

Even without John in the family tree, the story of George and Christiana would be a tale sufficient unto itself. They were American pioneers. It was before the Civil War that as a young couple they traveled, in all probability by foot and with only an ox-pulled wooden cart of their possessions, all the way from the mountains of Pennsylvania to their new home in central Ohio. Scrappy and adventurous, George was the quintessential American entrepreneur. He had a lifelong pattern of going after economic opportunity and finding success. His era was one of turmoil yet he seemed to surf the waves of social and commercial change. He and his wife lived to a very old age. After their deaths, John's wife's sister married the father of a sitting President of the United States, so I can say: John's life stretched from a dirt farm to the White House.

At the end of one visit to my Florida cousin, with my bags packed and one foot out of the door on my way to the airport, she found another cache of old family photos. There were delicious morsels among them. One picture we both exclaimed over was a formal pose of a group of six women. Together Deb and I recognized Minnie, John's wife and so by relative-age we thought we could together identify the others, Minnie's daughter Mae (Deb's grandmother), John's sister Emma and her daughter Beryl and a little boy who appears in other photos but whose identity remains a mystery. My guess is he is Beryl's son. In the center, like a stabilizing sun, is Christiana. I know it must be her! I can see my dad's eyes on her face. The photo shows a round, good-sized woman, not a beauty but comfortably attractive, so that when standing beside her tall and slender husband, they must have looked like the number 10.

In the 1880 Darke County census, twenty-year-old John is listed as a worker in a spoke factory ("wk spoke fctry") living in his father's household. In other words he made wooden spokes for wheels. In a world before plastic and automobiles when most everything was made of wood, the Lambert company made those spokes but their mainstay products were the long wooden poles and shafts which were used to hold the horse to the carriage. A shaft was either of two long pieces of wood between which a single horse is hitched to a wagon or carriage. A pole, also called a tongue, was a shaft that extended from the front axle of a wagon between the two horses closest to the wheels and by which the wagon was drawn. It is easy to imagine the advantage of flexible yokes, poles and shafts for the animals' comfort and the driver's control. The Lamberts of Union became known for their "bent wood," a woodworking technique involving steaming, sometimes soaking, and bending pieces of wood. Are not our bentwood chairs of today sturdy, beautiful and comfortable? The bentwood, aside from being aesthetically pleasing, gave flexibility and strength to the joints and to the greater wood construction of the poles and shafts. Records of the local 1885 census for Darke County show a listing for "JW Lambert and Company, handle manufacturer." Add to the list of Lambert products wooden handles for tools.

Throughout the next twenty years there will be many different names for the Lambert enterprises: The Union Manufacturing Company, The Buckeye Manufacturing Company, The Lambert Gas and Gasoline Engine Company, The Union Automobile Company, The Lambert Automobile Company and The Lambert

Motor Truck Company. There were other names that had no actual enterprise behind them. The names tell a story of an everychanging manufacturing effort. I believe the Buckeye Manufacturing Company with John as President and its production of gasoline engines was what we would consider the parent or flagship company; it stayed in existence as others came and went. I have seen a letterhead, perhaps saved for this reason, that shows John as President, George (the father) as Vice President, and George Albert, the oldest brother as Secretary/Treasurer. They list their products, "Hardware and Carriage Specialties". The marketplace was a wild territory back then with little safeguards for difficulty during economic downturns. The Lamberts were resourceful and were able to adjust to produce what could be sold. Their workers were loyal; most stayed with them for many years, even relocating to Indiana when the move was made. Records show that George opened his plant in Union employing six men and perhaps as many neighborhood boys. There were no child labor laws. In their peak car-manufacturing year the Lamberts had three, perhaps six hundred employees.

Descriptions of John in the automobile factory describe his always wearing a three-pieced suit. More often than not by the end of the day he had taken his jacket off, rolled up his sleeves and gotten involved on the factory floor. I believe John loved this part of his enterprise. He always remained "hands on" with the factory operation and gladly did most of the road testing himself. He was the one usually to handle customer complaints. He had a close working relationship with his men. I believe he loved the dirt and the noise, the clanking of metal tools and creating something from various pieces and then the success of improved machines.

This was the era of the Labor Movement, but unionizing did not make the family history. George and his sons were able to provide enough to keep the unions out which having heard my father talk, I am sure this was their goal. My impression is that those old Lamberts had a fundamental respect for a worker who applied him/herself and the workers knew it. At least I want to think so. Dan Davis collected an old story from a factory worker who remembered in 1916 the workers had threatened to strike at the Buckeye plant in Anderson. Their pay at the time was 17 1/2 cents an hour; they asked for 19. When they approached John he told them that their current wage was better than what was had by any shop in town, which was probably true, and that he would "shut 'er down" before he would pay such an outrageous wage. The men did strike, but started drifting back after a time until the strike was broken. Dan notes all his interviews included fond memories of John Lambert with several calling him generous and honest. Child labor laws forbidding employment of young children did not come until 1920. Young boys were until then an integral part of factory work. Since George and Christiana themselves produced so many young boys who no doubt worked at the factory, I am hoping that exonerates him from his taking advantage of another family's young sons. My dad is quick to say, the boys clamored for the positions of employment at the plant.

The factory the father of ten built in Union was innovative for his time in that he pulled together under one roof processes that previously were done in separate facilities. Without electricity, natural lighting was the order of the day and George's brick building had unusually large windows and carefully positioned sunny exposures. He picked a site for his facilities eight miles from home near the "union" of three railroads in the Village of Union, which straddles two state lines Indiana and Ohio. On one side of Union's main street, where the railroads met, is Indiana; the other side is Ohio. In George's day rail lines ended at the state line and passengers were obliged to disembark before reboarding on the other side of the border to continue their journey. This was the impetus for Union's inception and growth. Today citizens of Union City schedule their lives with two different time zones which they differentiate "fast time" and "slow time." A resident explained, "The plumbing around Union City is like the school kids – one set goes east and one set goes west."

John and his siblings attended the County High School in Union City for two recorded years. Although he married a woman with some college education and both their children graduated from college, those two years were all the formal education that The Genius in my family had. Although public education was not available then as we enjoy it today, those early Lamberts were critical thinkers, self-educated, literate and knowledgeable of the world around them.

In the 1880's the Wright Brother's maternal grandfather John Koerner had a carriage-making business outside of Greenville a few miles from Union. Perhaps when the young brothers Orville and Wilbur visited their grandfather from their home in Dayton, Ohio they may have gotten to know the somewhat older Lambert boys Al and JW whose father had a similar business. There is no record but it is certainly possible. The Wright Brothers inherited their mechanical aptitude from their mother who no doubt received it from her Saxon-born blacksmith father John Koerner. I grew up in Dayton within a half mile of the Wright Brother's mansion Hawthorne Hill. One of the largest and most beautiful homes in town, it sits in Georgian splendor atop a high, sloping hill. I remember playing as a young girl on its clovered lawn and climbing in its maple trees. One evening each Christmastime the town's elementary schoolchildren would be gathered at the top of the hill at twilight to sing carols. More than the singing I remember they gave us coconut macaroons and hot chocolate slathered with melting marshmallows. I passed the Wright mansion daily as I walked to and from school.

For reasons known only as family legends John left Union, his family, the house and factory at age twenty-four and moved by himself fifty miles away to a small Ohio farm town called Enterprise. What a great name for a home for this brilliant young man at this point in America's history! John bought and ran a lumberyard north of Enterprise. Among that last cache of pictures of John's birth family, my cousin and I found an astonishing old photograph that must be the John Lambert lumberyard. The picture shows the care the men took knowing their images were to be taken; they had donned top hats! Perhaps in addition to George's timberland in a southern (unspecified) state, the family out-posted John in Van Wert County to supply the Union City business with wood. There are no records to reconstruct this part of the story. As well as the lumberyard, John owned a granary on the railroad in town to which he added a grain mill. These were lucrative businesses and showed his knack for collecting a profit. Perhaps this financial independence was what drew our hero to strike out on his own. Or perhaps it had something to do with romance. I don't know. He moved to Enterprise in 1884. It is in this setting, away from his family and thriving on his own, that he built America's first car.

John's father would have seen the several converging factors for economic potential in Enterprise and encouraged his son to make the move. The town of Enterprise was a major railroad crossing, just like where George had earlier relocated his family and settled in Union. This was before trucking, so goods were shipped by railroad or boat. Transportation services are always critical for commerce and back then railroad stops quickly became important merchant centers.

The Lambert family in association with the successful Parent family surely knew that serving farmers was a solid business. A granary was almost impervious to economic downturns, for people always need to eat. John's granary milled some of the grain into flour and collected the rest in a silo beside the railroad tracks. From there it could be loaded directly into a boxcar by opening a chute to allow the grain to flow into the top of the storage rail car and thus efficiently sent to markets in Toledo, Columbus and Springfield, Dayton and Cincinnati, Ft. Wayne and Chicago. The side of John's building boasted the words: *JW Lambert and Company, Will Buy All Kinds of Grains and Seeds. Flour exchanged for wheat. Exchange and grinding a specialty. Chop food for sale. Cash for Grain.*

John also owned the town hardware store, which in those days meant he sold items farmers might need, from large farm equipment down to hand tools. That building displayed the letters: *Lambert Hall, Harvesting Machinery, ASPA and ACL Implements and Buggies and Waggons (sic)*. I imagine the hardware store as being John's personal tool shed with all the latest popular gadgets for farm and town laid out for his musing and use. Rather quickly he built and owned the Town Hall and Opera House as well as the town jail. I can envision Mr. and Mrs. Lambert dressed to the nines as they attend a program in their own theater. Minnie had strong opinions about what was proper viewing, so the program they would attend, I am sure, had been carefully screened, maybe a poetry reading by the young Dayton poet Paul Dunbar, or a lecture on history, a spelling bee or a political recitation. Maybe Minnie's childhood neighbor Phoebe Moses came to perform with her husband Frank Butler. She had lived in proximity to the Kelley family during the dire years of the Civil War. It is likely Phoebe who, as an eight year old supported her own family shooting game, also helped the Kelleys survive. Both sharpshooters were entertainers with Wild Bill Hickok's traveling show; the public knew her as Annie Oakley. I can imagine the two couples sharing a meal in the Lambert's Enterprise home. With no television or motion pictures, traveling entertainment shows were the center of public entertainment. In the few years John lived in Enterprise, he made some major contributions to his adopted community and did very well indeed. By thirty years of age, he had become a prominent citizen and lived with his young family in a nice home on Banner Street near the center of town.

I doubt John's success in Ohio City, as Enterprise is now named, made him afraid of complacency. He had achieved goals that would satisfy most men. He was successful and respected at home and in his commercial career overseeing and managing his businesses. On the contrary, with his mind ever blossoming, this busy man found time to retreat to the work shed he had set up for himself so he could tinker and invent. John had a lifelong pattern of re-working mechanical objects he encountered in life. He was motivated, his daughter said in a 1969 interview, by wanting to make things run better. He would often see a different way to accomplish a task and so retreated to his shed to construct what his inventive mind imagined.

Records in Ohio City show that in the six years John Lambert was a resident he bought eleven properties, all of which were sold when he left town. Why did he buy them? Perhaps the answer is as investments. He knew the town would be expanding and he was looking for more profit. Or perhaps his real estate dealings were in part motivated by wanting to stimulate that expansion. Or maybe his family with his numerous siblings wanted to join him in Van Wert County. The name on the deeds was always John Lambert. No other Lamberts of Union were ever registered as citizens but the census, which comes only every ten years, may have missed their tenure.

The other new citizen of distinction in Enterprise whose name was also on those deeds (but as a woman's, legally useless) was John's bride. He married Mary Francis ("Minnie") Kelley on July 5, 1885 in her home near Ansonia, a farm town north of Greenville then called Dallas. She was 24; John was 25. Minnie's father was a medical doctor and kept a modest household in an area of Darke County populated largely by people of French descent, people whose grandparents would tell of fleeing France in disappointment over Napoleon's failure to implement democracy. Dr. Kelley was the grandson of French immigrants. In some areas nearby French was still spoken but not in the Kelley household. Minnie was a fervent Methodist. Minnie's mother, born in Ohio like her father, boasted an English-born Revolutionary War hero in her family. Minnie's maternal great-grandfather Henry Horn fought against King George and must have been a source of great pride, for Minnie became a member of the Daughters of the American Revolution right after it was started in 1902, an emblem for which adorns her grave. Likely the union of John and Minnie was a matter of mutual pride to the two families. They seem well paired.

The course of their marriage was characterized by Minnie's strong personality and John's powerful intellect.

Both of John's parents were descendants of German immigrants. George's father Mike Lambert, according to a census report in the Greenville Library, was born in Prussia, now a part of Germany and would have immigrated through Philadelphia at the time so many left the tyrannical rule of the Lutheran State to find religious freedom in America, around 1820. Or perhaps as my Dad suggested, they came seeking higher profits. Alas, my Lambert surname is German. PBS did a show a few years ago on Americans of German descent which said sixty million Americans share a German heritage. Even that number sounds low and may only reflect those who openly celebrate October fest, beer and accordion music. I think sometime during the last century, even before Hitler, many German-Americans like the Lamberts put their lederhosen away and, identifying as Americans, stopped talking about the old connections. My Dad was not aware of his name's etiology. In fact he assumed the derivation was French. (Monsieur Lahm-bear) When I told him what I had discovered that our Lambert is a German name, he said, "Maybe that's why my Dad was called 'Dutch.'" "Deutch" yes, indeed!

About the wedding of John and Minnie, there is one reported fact that is startling: the bride wore black! In her day, it was the fashion to choose from any number of colored gowns and she would refer over the years to the practicality of her black taffeta. And black it was! John and his bride were a devoted couple; his large frame brought him the nickname T-Rex while his tiny wife was aptly named Minnie (was she even 5'2"?). Methodists at the time were known for being a finger-pointing, disapproving, meddling kind of group. There were no family stories to that extreme, but her rules and her dominion of the family home are legendary. She disapproved of dancing, drinking any alcohol ever and of effervescent drinks which were ban from the house. There was no ice cream or comics on Sundays. Common and controversial at the time, spitting was out of the question around Minnie and probably John, too. He did not chew tobacco like so many men did, but preferred a more genteel pipe or an occasional cigar. Cigarette smoking was considered effeminate in men and grossly improper in women. In their later years, Minnie allowed John only one cigar a day which explains the photo of him puffing on a two-foot cigar. If John wanted to enjoy the newfangled drink called Coca-Cola, Minnie barred the behavior to the back porch. When radio technology ushered in household radios, Minnie resisted; I would not be surprised to have found John's in his work shed. So the story goes. Probably a man like him needed an organized, slightly compulsive partner like Minnie. Although her suspicious safeguarding may seem ridiculous now, the scrubbing of body and home and the selective protection of what enters the home had a positive function of discouraging germs for common infections that in this time before penicillin could easily lead to death. Modern descendants may giggle at the stories of Minnie's extreme standards but part of what she was doing may have ensured my mere presence.

As John became successful and his business led him to travel extensively, Minnie preferred to stay at home. Although their letters are gone, there is a box of postcards that is evidence of daily correspondence over their absences, even without long distance telephone or any Internet services. This collection is part of what I found in Florida. Along with a spoon collection, the postcards tell something of their travels including a California tour Minnie made with Ray and Dorothy his young bride, my grandmother. Their words to each other, written where others can see, are formal. But their words also tell of the cordial devotion between the inventive genius and his wife. If his wife did not endorse all of her husband's pursuits, she heartily supported the lifestyle he expected. She was fastidious, yes, but had gracious taste in her home making. The objects that are left are opulent Victorian pieces. Sadly, so much of the household items were lost because the home was broken up so many years after John and Minnie's heyday. John was lucky to have a wife who steadfastly upheld her responsibilities providing a home and in raising their children. I consider her quite lucky as well. My great-grandmother reportedly never liked automobiles but in later years she willingly joined her husband on weekly trips to the theater to watch the latest installment of Tom Edison's moving picture serials. Their marriage lasted until Minnie's death in 1949, sixty-four years. John was a widower for three years. He maintained a private religious life and was a practical Protestant, meaning he worshiped with a convenient neighborhood congregation and at the time of his death was affiliated with the Presbyterian Church. Their two children Mae (1886) and Ray (1888) were born during their Enterprise years. My great grandfather was only thirty when he built the first car.

Chapter 3

Early Advances

In 1876 a middle-aged mechanic in Europe, Nicholas Otto, invented his four-stroke internal combustion engine. This was the first gasoline engine that actually ran. Today (still) almost all of our cars and trucks are powered by his principles. No wonder we came to call our cars "otto-mobiles". Using two cycles of the crankshaft, the four-stroke principle provides more balance to the engine block than a two-stroke engine, which was common at the time. These are the concepts John fell in love with. As the flywheel begins its turn, the piston pulls a mixture of gasoline and air into an internal chamber, then as the flywheel completes the first cycle, the piston pressurizes the mixture and the next down turn fires the fuel, which drives the piston down again and the exhausted fuel mixture is ejected from the cylinder. As the process continues, the gear shafts rotate converting piston combustion to rotary energy. The attractive idea here was generating power. The choice to use gasoline was secondary to the goal of creating useable energy.

During the 1880's, Europeans Gottlieb Daimler and Karl Benz experimented with combining Otto's new little gasoline engine with bicycles and carriages. With crude methods involving cumbersome leather belts, the engine on their model could transmit a force to make a wheel turn. Germans, it was said, fathered the automobile and the French rocked the cradle. The French had the best roads and so were the most hospitable to the commercial success of the horseless carriage. Still, when in 1886 Karl Benz made a go of production and offered his hand-built self-propelled gasoline vehicles for sale, public interest was low and sales were sparse.

Seventy-five miles from Union, Ohio a man in Indianapolis, Indiana purchased one of the Benz vehicles and it became a focal point for curious citizens far and wide. An Otto engine was displayed at the Chicago Exposition in 1893. Both internal combustion machines appeared in relatively close proximity to where John was living but I have no idea if he saw either of them. There is no reference to these two events in family records.

In contrast, mentioned often in family records is a fortuitous trip John made with his father, also in 1876. Perhaps this trip more than anything else provided for the boy a vision of breakthrough possibilities. The experience of seeing a little engine with no boiler planted a seed that grew to a mental tool and eventually John conceptualized his self-propelled car. On a visit to a tannery to drop off hides, George Lambert saw an amazing sight, a little boilerless engine operating some machinery. Perhaps in this area of Ohio rich with French immigrants the tanner had connections in France, which is where this engine was likely manufactured, for it was one of the very first to use gasoline as fuel. When George got home he told his son about the unusual little power source. John asked to accompany his father when he returned to pick up his tanned hides so he could witness this new technology. George recognized and supported his son's unique interests. On the return trip, father and son were dismayed to learn the tanner had suffered a fire that engulfed the engine and JW would not be able to see what it could do. But dismay turned to curiosity when the tanner invited the sixteen-year-old to dig the little engine out of the warm rubble. Young John Lambert, who would later hold dozens of patents related to the gasoline engine including the first patent for a complete gasoline engine, had the unique opportunity to see up close a rare slide-valve coal gas engine. He could, by a twist of fate, put its parts in his hands. John "tore it to pieces" Ray writes, and thus the inventor gained his first knowledge of a type of engine that did not require a boiler. It was a peak experience for the curious young man and left an impression that lasted a lifetime. The idea of obtaining power from a gasoline engine small enough to be portable fascinated John so he was immediately interested when he heard of the developments for a horseless carriage in Europe some ten years later.

In John's day horses were beloved and revered. They were members of the family and supplied valued help both for work and transportation. Horsepower was the order of the day. But the animals also had to be fed and housed. Plus, each horse left behind up to thirty pounds of manure a day! That's a lot of hay and a pollution problem, for the time, impossible to overcome. It created dust that fouled the air, which resulted in respiratory and intestinal infections. In 1890 approximately 15,000 dead horses were abandoned on the streets of New York City, commonly left for days, aggravating traffic and health hazards. Problems with the horse were obvious at the time and individualized mechanical means of getting around definitely had caught the public's attention by the end of the nineteenth century.

As personal transportation evolved, in the time between the horse and the automobile there was the brief eminence of the bicycle. The bicycle was the stepping-stone between walking and driving a car. Family records indicate the Lamberts were enthusiastic about using the new human-powered machines. The idea for mechanical bicycles came from children's toys. The toy horse, or hobbyhorse, became the precursor to the bicycle. Europeans led development of what we would eventually recognize as a bicycle. The early hobbyhorse sometimes had two back wheels and was a tricycle; others were two-wheeled bicycles. Both two- and three-wheeled models of human and mechanical propulsion machines were common right through the turn of the nineteenth century. The first official bike, in 1865, was called the "Boneshaker" for obvious reasons. Rubber tires soon followed. The Ordinary of the 1870's had the comically large front wheel and, with a high center of gravity for the rider, was very dangerous. It is where the phrase "taking a header" comes from. As the quality of steel improved, new designs were possible. The Safety of 1885 had a strong and practical shape and sold like hotcakes. Bicycle riding became a craze. Americans were on the move. By 1896, over four hundred manufacturers produced two million bikes for a population of 65 million. I bet George Lambert made notes as he watched bicycle-makers reap their profits.

Another invention of the time also radically effected daily routines. Americans were staying up past dark. Thomas Edison patented the light bulb in 1879 and by mid-1880's, he had developed the power plant to make electricity available to industry and the public. The Village of Ohio City got street lamps run by electricity in 1884.

Before the Safety, in 1888, the year of Ray Lambert's birth, the idea of a motorized self-propelled vehicle being of any use to the people of the county was purely speculative, considered ridiculous by some and simply a daydream by others. Most people got around on foot. Long distances were traveled by train and when possible, by boat. Before any Highway Act, roads were rutted and muddy; very few were paved, the pavement being logs, bricks or crushed rocks. Except for the extremely rich, people did not travel distances except for grand or desperate occasions. Acquiring bicycles opened up possibilities in the thinking of local Americans about getting around. Boundaries fell back as people contemplated further destinations and indeed, traveled greater distances as a matter of routine. Travel became dramatically more widespread and created a national experience that was the groundwork for the introduction and acceptance of the automobile with its dramatic ability to extend those boundaries by a giant leap.

Early wheelmen, as bicycle riders called themselves, broke the ice for the automobile. They lobbied for better roads and for access to those roads. They withstood the hostility of those who resisted change and fought attitudes that would curb or ban riding. Too many folks were participating to be held back. The commercial success of the craze was spurred by greed for speed. Bike racing became an industry and was very popular. The champion celebrity of the day was a black American from Indianapolis and later Worcester, Massachusetts named Marshall W. "Major" Taylor who by 1898 held seven world records. This widespread outbreak of speed lust was a prelude to auto racing.

Early in the Wright Brothers' career they were in the bicycle business. A lot of the early car makers like the Duryea brothers of Massachusetts and Ransom Olds of Michigan entered the industry from carriage or bicycle making, but not exclusively. Others of the early automotive leaders included the son of a railroad magnate and another of a gun maker, immigrants (Louis Chevrolet and his two brothers, race stars Arthur and Gaston) and farm boys (Henry Ford and John Lambert). John is called a farm boy or former farm boy in many articles, including in his obituary. There are many sources that describe John's ability to get along with a wide spectrum of people, from a low-level company worker to the leaders of industry. He was a farm boy and the son of a successful carriage maker.

It was while my great-grandparents lived in Enterprise that John designed his prototype self-propelled vehicle. He built a sophisticated, mechanically successful buggy. How I wish I knew more about his process as he devised and developed his complicated dream. If only I could have been a fly on the wall of his work shed! I would like to have observed what he did and also what his attitude was. How confident in 1890 could he have been that anyone would buy his machine? The bicycle craze was soaring but roads were poor and prejudices were tough. It was wild speculation on John's part to imagine his new fangled idea could be a successful product. I know he was confident about accomplishing the mechanics. I think he believed if he could sell a few mechanically proficient models, they would be their own advertisement and help generate further sales. I can't reconstruct his state of mind but certain elements of his circumstances I can vouch for.

He had easy access to all the tools and pieces he would need from the factory in Union. He was already an experienced engineer, draftsman and inventor. By this time his father's company was building wagon and carriage chassis. John must have been involved in that end of things, if not in charge altogether. The prototype of his original car shows advanced engineering skills. I picture his doing his experimenting and building in private. Reports tell of the hardware store being the private setting of the first trial runs. It was customary for inventors of the time to conceal their tinkering activities. No one wanted their idea stolen or laughed at. Competition for good ideas was fierce. Perhaps John Lambert moved to Enterprise to have anonymity and privacy to work on this project, which surely must have been an exciting prospect, rumors of which would draw a lot of interest.

I don't know if John included his extended family in what he was doing. Their involvement is first mentioned in any records as being just before the new little gasoline engine ran the buggy for the first time. Ray writes that John's father and a brother (unidentified) had "become immensely interested" and describes their visit to Enterprise not until the engine successfully ran. It's hard to imagine that his father at least was not in on the activities going on behind closed doors up in Enterprise. The others surely recognized John as an inventor even if they did not know the specifics of his project. John had demonstrated his ability to come up with unique and practical solutions to make and improve tools and machines for years. Maybe he talked openly about his vision of a self-propelled vehicle; no reports survive.

John was not the only one with visions of a horseless carriage. Newspaper stories of the day told of other prototypes for self-propelled vehicles. There were models using steam power and electric battery power, some of which actually ran and could be seen on the streets of America, i.e. the Stanley, the Locomobile, and the Electrobat. Others tried sails, gunpowder, rubber bands and various far-fetched propulsion schemes. But those others did not work and of those that did, there were major difficulties. Battery- and steam-powered vehicles enjoyed some years of commercial viability, but although silent, electric cars had no pull and soon ran out of charge; and steam, with its boiling water and pressurized compartments, was just too dangerous to gain lasting popular acceptance. These methods could not compete in popularity with the horse, although experimental contraptions proliferated. John likely saw local experiments for self-propelled vehicles that used steam and electricity. A man in Greenville was one of the first to build a horseless carriage. He devised it by putting a stationary steam engine on a carriage meant to be pulled by a horse. It was an attention-getter! But it was not useful. The ride was too dangerous, unmanageable and cumbersome.

Mounting a stationary engine on a vehicle designed to be pulled by a horse was the predominate plan of most self-propelled pioneers. They would then have to concoct a method of transmission to fit the machines to bring the power to turn the wheels. It is to be noted John did not do this. He was first to integrate the engine, transmission and chassis into one design. He designed and built a buggy that would carry the weight of the engine, a buggy intended to be self-propelled rather than pulled. His engine was designed and built to be portable.

In 1937, Ray devised a list of questions that he submitted to his father. Creating this document was one of many substantial contributions Ray made in John's retirement years (retired from car-making, not inventing) in his quest to establish his father's credentials as the first car maker to devise a gas-propelled automobile. John's answers reveal him to have been a man of few words. Although his answers are brief, he gave valuable insight to his process. Much of my understanding of my great-grandfather's accomplishment comes from these four pages in which he reflects over forty years. John remembered being aware before he built his original car of the experiments in Europe. Perhaps his German-born grandfather pointed them out to encourage the young inventor's imagination. John read about Nicholas Otto's work with a four stroke, three-cylinder gasoline engine and became a believer in the supremacy of this four-stroke pattern. He knew about Karl Benz's three-wheeled car in Mannheim from an 1889 issue of *Scientific American*. John had his own intuition about what would work best on a self-propelled buggy. That intuition was embellished by curiosity and tempered by his experience as a mechanic on the farm and at the factory.

Karl Benz had built a vehicle powered with a gasoline engine. Dazzled though John must have been by what he read in 1889, when he looked over the illustrations, as was his habit he saw a way to do it better. John's criticism of Benz's vehicle was that it was "heavy." Benz used wide leather straps that required large metal tensioners or braces to move power from the gears to the wheels; John saw this design as weighty, cumbersome and inefficient.

Lightness was a concept John wed early. This is counter-intuitive to the way we think today. Today, we look to buy heavy cars because we want a smooth ride and the sense of protection. But in John's day, before paved roads, carriages were built to be light and flexible for the ride to be smooth and for the mechanics to last. Likely first developed as a trademark quality at his father's factory, lightness remained a benchmark tenet throughout John's career. Long before the invention of the shock absorber, the Lamberts were involved in developing the flexibility of vehicles by using bentwood parts for its elasticity and give. Early bentwood configurations were in fact early shock absorbers. The rule for lightness was applied not only to John's first prototype, but also later to the cars the family produced under John's engineering guidance, 1902-1917. Those Lambert cars were certifiably advertised and praised for the lightness of their overall design along with their elegance and mechanical strength.

John' first prototype was flexible and sturdy and surprisingly light. Ray illustrates John's dedication to lightness with an example. (In order to achieve lightness)... "He went to such extremes as having a crankcase enclosed by means of a case built by a manufacturer in Cleveland who took burlap and formed it as a crankcase cover and treated it through some process of his own to make it oil proof and oil tight." Ever hear of a burlap crankcase cover? John designed a sturdy car with simple, thin lines. The height of the driver's seat, the size of the wheels, as well as the parts of the chassis, engine and body all added to the aura and reality of being airy and light.

Advancements in steel production precipitously happened to John's schedule. By 1890 lighter, stronger steel was being forged in Cleveland and was within easy access to Enterprise. John had several items that he used on the original car constructed in Cleveland because they were not produced locally in small towns, including parts of the engine and gears, and the upholstery including the surried top. With its large store of natural gas and the convenience of Lake Erie, Cleveland was a bustling center of commerce.

During the time John was in Enterprise, carriage makers in Michigan and elsewhere were pioneering clever uses for the newly developed steel-coiled spring to absorb shock from uneven road surfaces and to keep wagons and carriages level. The problem of keeping an even keel when carrying an uneven load was an engineering challenge, for passengers and cargo could be dumped on a turn. John adapted their concepts for using heavy springs to his project to augment dexterity and create as smooth a ride as possible. When asked by Ray, "What was your belief regarding mounting a motor transmission . . .?" John's reply was short: "Everything on springs."

The transmission design of John's first automobile prototype involved two clutches and two chains which gave two forward speeds. This transfer of power was clever. Chains from the engine's crankshaft to the rear axle forced the wheels to turn. John had developed a unique bevel type gear that he used on the rear axle, a sophisticated innovation at the time, which provided a smooth transition at start-up and between gears. The small single front wheel was directed by a foot lever, probably shaped like rabbit ears, for each foot to press in different directions. The car was steered by foot! This method proved to be tiresome, so John immediately added springs. Later he added a hand-held tiller to help direct the front little wheel. John's three-wheeled design was simpler than a four-wheeled model and followed Benz's decision to use the common-for-the-time three wheels.

There is no record of John's time while he worked on his design and built his prototype. Would it have been years? Or just months? My guess is he began his project in earnest in 1890. As he read and tinkered and drew designs, was he silent in his obsession or cheerful about his creativity? I wonder if he had squirreled ideas away for years to apply to a horseless carriage or if they came up for him unbidden as he worked on his prototype. My educated guess is that like his vehicle his mood was light and he was solidly purposeful with his time and thinking. There is a consistency to his personality from all descriptions I have collected of his being a contented, pleasant, self-contained person, a hard worker with an immense attention span. One idiosyncratic specific I know: John favored onions. I saw a postcard Minnie sent him of a California onion field on which she writes, "Because I know how you like onions..."

I imagine JW in his work shed throughout the year 1890. Often with the smell of onions on his breath, that of oil absorbed into the packed dirt floor and of the kerosene he no doubt burned to light his project and heat the room, he toiled as so many would-be inventors did in similar workshops across Ohio, Michigan, Indiana and the entire nation, each eager to come up with an item that would explode on the nation's consciousness, lift up the suffering masses and bring riches and fame to themselves, or at least some degree of security in an economy without protections to escape poverty and starvation. I think John was motivated by his own curiosity as well as his desire to provide for the larger Lambert family enterprise. As a teenager he saw his corn planter give enormous help to farmers; perhaps the humanitarian in him hoped to replicate that. The wheels, chassis and body were familiar constructions to this man. The engine he envisioned was in his imagination only; John needed to keep his eyes open until he found what he needed. Once John acquired the engine, the onions, oil and kerosene would mix with the smell of gasoline. While Minnie fretted over the possibilities that introduced, I can visualize John working late into the night tackling the problems of balance and stability, comfort and durability, stop and go. He was making manifest his vision of a practical machine that would transport its riders without the aid of a horse.

Chapter 4

1891 and The Original Car

When I was eight years old, my family moved from one house to a much larger home about a mile away in the same town. A few times after the move, we went as a family to visit our former neighbors. One such occasion was memorable for the one-on-one moment I had with my busy father. While the others were occupied elsewhere, he took me by the hand across the Parkers' driveway. We ducked around some bushes to enter the backyard next door. Mrs. Parker's elderly mother lived here. I knew my Dad was excited and that taking me was an excuse to go himself. Whatever was inside that garage I could tell was mighty important to him. He had me stand where the large wooden door would first open which gave me the best view while he unlatched the hinge at the side. It was an old style garage door hanging on a rail, so my Dad had to slide the whole thing out of the way. The car had been backed in, so the first I saw of it was its face. It was not the brass headlights or the cute side lanterns that initially caught my eye, but the tall narrow wheels and the height at which the car sat. At my size of four-feet-something, it mattered. The wheels were high and the thin tires grabbed my attention. They were a cross between a car tire and a tire for my bike. I had never seen an antique car before.

At first glance the car appeared skinny. Without an enclosed compartment for the riders, it was much more open than present day models and so looked to have not much meat on its bones. To my eight-year-old eyes, accustomed to Impalas and Fairlanes, this looked like a car in high heels, all dressed up. It was tall and bare-boned but jeweled. The brass was rich and generously appeared in lots of places. I knew by instinct not to speak aloud to my father while he was first looking at the car. His enthusiasm filled up the entire interior of the building. He spoke but not particularly to me declaring what a beautiful and unique machine it was. He was enchanted with the pretty little car. To my observations it looked delicate which I might have said to him and if I did, I know now he would have scoffed. He no doubt described to me what a strong machine it was, the loads it could haul and the inclines it could climb. I remember his explaining he was storing the car in Mrs. Dill's garage until he could "get it worked on." And I remember his attention being absorbed in examining every inch of it. He pulled up the seat cushions and looked under them, and then he touched the pedals and levers by the steering wheel which to my eyes was on the wrong side. He swung the little door to the backseat open and closed to check the latch. The movement was smooth and secure. He pulled open the hood which unfolded up on the side while I poked at some bugs crawling in the dirt. Perhaps I showed some boredom. It didn't stop him from gazing for some time at whatever it was that made up the engine under the hood. He fiddled with what he was looking at. He was interactive with the vehicle while I did not attempt to put my fingers on it at all. Before we left, he bent to one knee to see the bottom of the car and craned his neck to see back under the chassis.

Standing, he took my hand and we stepped away. Before turning to go, we admired the old car sitting there all tucked safely out of the world's way. I remember agreeing with him about how attractive it looked in the old wooden garage. Dad pulled the hanging door shut. Mrs. Dill's driveway had not been used in years so the garage had a feel of being alone and out of the way especially to a little girl. It might have been late September, with golden light in the air coming through half-naked trees and the beginning of leaf piles collecting in the yard. As we walked back to meet the other members of the family, I remember quite clearly my father stating that the car I had just witnessed in that garage was a part of our family and connected to me because it was built by his grandfather.

The pretty little car in Mrs. Dill's garage made a vivid impression on me and still holds a presence in my mind. I use this memory to imagine John's father George's reaction in January 1891 as he stood before an opened door in Ohio City and saw for the first time his son's completed creation. About a half century later, John's son Ray tried to reconstruct the moment on paper. Ray wrote a three thousand-word essay describing the inception of his father's invention that starts with specifics in December 1890.

It was in this month that a John B. Hicks of Cleveland, Ohio applied for American patents on a stationary gasoline engine. John traveled probably by train to Cleveland, home of JD Rockefeller's Standard Oil, to meet Mr. Hicks where he obtained a license to use Hicks' patents that stated John's engine would be used "only on land vehicles other than railway or tramway cars." Perhaps like many newspaper editors and civic leaders of the day, Mr. Hicks visualized the future of transportation using gasoline engines to fuel mass transit systems, replacing the electric street railways then in use, and mocked the idea of individuals using motorcars. Gasoline engines were in common use in America only on boats, for maritime purposes and the next step the developers saw was to apply this power source for mass urban transit or for public travel over land between urban centers. John was planning to apply Mr. Hick's patents to individual land vehicles and Mr. Hicks had no objections. With the license in hand, John could design an engine to his own specifications. Mr. Hicks got John in touch with a former employee, a German immigrant architectural engineer who could in his spare time oversee the making of the component parts John designed. This modified Hicks three-cylinder engine was John's first experience in designing a gasoline engine. Initially, John paid Mr. William Wacholtz $200 to work on his project. That quickly grew to $3,300 and still the engine was not running. John had the machine shipped from Mr. Wacholtz's shop in the Lowell Machine Works in Cleveland to a small machine shop in Van Wert, six miles from Enterprise. Ray wrote about acquiring the new engine, "This did not cover a long period of time, but was a rapid development." With it, John set out to complete America's original (portable) gasoline automobile engine.

Once in his possession, John needed to get his engine running. He needed a method of firing the engine. Coincidentally he read about a boat newly arrived on the East Coast from Europe that had a Daimler engine, so he traveled all the way to New York City to view the engine on the boat in the harbor there to learn Daimler's method of carburetion. He was able to ascertain the general idea that a vapor was made by mixing air with a small amount of the gasoline. Because John could not learn Daimler's specific process, he came home to figure out a way of his own. He developed what he called a "vaporizer" and within days (yes, days) his vehicle was in operation. John was confident the parts of his dream would fit together as he had planned. "This vaporizer was a simple affair," Ray tells us, "wherein he drew the air past the gasoline, picked the gasoline up in the proper proportions, produced the vapor to go into the cylinders, and with a make or break ignition he fired the charge."

The vaporizer was clever and involved a series of chambers; John's patent for it was one of the first carburetor patents. It represents a patent from the first car. Even though John accomplished this tricky step in his project in a short time, he did not know when he set out that he would succeed so quickly. Nonetheless, this step distinguishes John as the sophisticated mechanical inventor that he was. He easily came up with a method for getting the fuel into the carburetor.

When he first tried to start up the engine he broke the outer end of the crankshaft, not once, but twice. Was he discouraged? He did not give up. Each time he solved the problem by removing a cylinder. This conveniently made the mechanics lighter, but really he did it because having the crankshaft rebuilt meant a return trip to Cleveland, an enormous and intolerable delay. He was in a hurry to accomplish this task. John must have been pleased when, with one cylinder functioning, the lighter engine ran true. With this and with his own carburetor and system of drives, John's engine went quite beyond the Hicks' patent.

At this point, before the entire car was assembled but with the engine working, Ray tells us, John sent for his father and a brother (my guess is Al) to witness the little power source with portable fuel. Upon their arrival in the middle of a cold winter night, they demanded to see what they had been told which John obliged. John took them to his work shed where he showed them the engine he had been working on. The single cylinder machine his father saw must have struck George as tiny indeed. He was skeptical so small a machine could generate enough power to move a vehicle. To test it George took a large elm plank and, balancing it on a fulcrum, used it to bear down on the flywheel. John gradually opened the throttle. The friction from the flywheel made the plank smoke but the mighty little engine kept up. George was convinced. He insisted John and the Union Manufacturing Company go into production together as soon as the vehicle was ready. Ray writes John agreed that night. I suspect that even at this early point the Lamberts knew they had a new product for distribution, for even without a vehicle around it the engine was an amazing thing. Little did they know the havoc that would be waged in the century to come to feed gasoline-burning machines.

From Ray's description of the continuing events, I think John's transmission was ready before he acquired his engine. Ray calls the final compilation of buggy and engine a rapid affair. John moved energy from the engine to the back wheel with chains, not belts as Karl Benz was using.

George no doubt had a pretty good idea of the completed project his son had in mind, but I doubt anything could have prepared him for what he was eventually to see. He and Al went home to Union while John returned to his work shed to assemble his project, to connect the working engine onto the body of the vehicle. As the father waited back at home to hear from his son in Enterprise, did he anticipate that moment with excitement, even glee? Or did he take a businessman's practical approach of believing John's success when he saw it?

Now that the engine was in running condition, John quickly secured it on the waiting vehicle. Within days, Ray tells us, the engine was mounted in its special place behind the seat of the stylish three-wheeled automobile.

I assume John took a test run before he called anyone else. So far his project had been done under lock and key. In order to maintain that secrecy, he rearranged the contents of his cavernous hardware store to make room for an indoor runway for the vehicle to maneuver. John had the farm implements pulled off to the side or closer to the middle of the floor to achieve a roundabout path. When the time came, I imagine John positioned the car so its first spurt of acceleration would be down a straight, cleared path into the large room. He must have done this in nighttime, for when else could he avoid the prying eyes of the daytime public? The dark windows were perhaps frosted, for it was shortly after Christmas. Ray tells us the "blinds were pulled down."

I can imagine the scene when John first held the handle of the crank nestled in his palm moments before he successfully made it go, standing, poised, ready to throw the first turn of the flywheel. I am confident he, with his mechanic's mind, took for granted all would work well and he would get his ride. When John twisted his shoulder to give effort to his thrust, did the eager little engine start right away or did it make the young inventor repeat his effort and work for his reward? Once the little powerhouse kicked in and the noise and the smoke started collecting, how long did it take John to spring to the driver's position? It is a deep pleasure to imagine the thirty-year-old businessman up on the buttoned leather seat, engine vibrating the entire sculpture, and to see him in my mind's eye as he moved the car around the implement store for the first time. Imagine the sound and the echo inside those four walls! Imagine the smoke, as the engine worked and the gasoline burned. How marvelous must he have felt, guiding that small front wheel over the smooth packed dirt floor by using levers at his feet, swaying with the chassis around the corners of the loop! I can almost feel my own body move to compensate for the turn of the vehicle inside that showroom. John no doubt pushed for speed even in so small a space. He was driving a car! As we used to say back in Ann Arbor, he was motor-vated!

Now was the time to contact his father and brother. Once bidden, the two men traveled back to Enterprise quickly, knowing they were to witness, in Ray's words, "something new under the sun." Like eight-year-old Carol, George would have stood in anticipation of what was inside as John unlatched the door to the implement store. The door opened and John's father got his first view. What was George struck by? George had seen a lot of contraptions in his day; did any beat what was before him now? Although not a child, would he have experienced some of the wonder I did? America's first automobile weighed only 560 pounds and was about as tall as he was. Visually pleasing, John's car was stylish and lush; this was a well-developed product. No doubt George did like what he saw. With not only an approving entrepreneur's eye to potential profit, the father must also have looked upon his clever son with pride.

Whether he expressed it or not, John surely enjoyed showing his machine to his family and friends. He had given his vehicle smart details. Having a top was unique and John's was surried. The seat and its back were covered with rich black leather neatly upholstered with buttons. On each side of the seat was a spindled bentwood armrest. The cushion of the car seat was removable to allow access under it. This is where John placed the gasoline tank, which he called the receiving tank. Yes, John rode around sitting on top of twelve gallons of gasoline! Think about that and you will begin to understand Minnie's reluctance. The board across the front of the driver's compartment had a practical purpose. Its weight helped balance the vehicle and it protected the driver from upturned rubble in the road. Like the back wheels, the grace of its design pleases the eye. The curve of its lines reflects the curve of the line of the armrests. It was likely made of metal, although possibly of wood. John's large back wheels were thin and made of steel; no rubber here. It was too new a technology. The sixteen wooden spokes on each are beautiful to the eye. This well thought out prototype was no stunt; it was designed to go into manufacture. This first vehicle, like his commercially successful vehicles of the following decade, was light in weight, mechanically reliable, a hard-working machine that was both stylish and comfortable.

Best of all, the thing ran! I presume the Lambert men immediately took turns driving, riding and examining this novelty in a gleeful mood, amazed and excited that the little engine actually moved the machine with driver and rider. John's obsession with lightness had paid off. His single cylinder engine, with its 3 ½" bore and 4" stroke was sufficient to drive his car. Ray tells us "a great many trips were made in this car on the floor of the implement house." Oh, really? Do boys like to play with their toys? "Yee Haw's" filled the air, I am sure. What a ride it must have been! While the car did its magic that first night the conversation, I surmise, turned fantastic. Although I think they were prepared, new possibilities had just opened up before these uneducated but clever men. As the smoke gathered in the enclosed space, could they begin to imagine the deeper ramifications of what this combination of steel and gasoline would bring to the world? Or imagine that as their descendent (me) wrote of that first night ever of riding a car using gasoline for fuel, I would be witnessing a world in crisis over its use? Whether they could image a far future or not, they focused on their opportunity. These Ohio businessmen no doubt discussed the feasibility of various ideas for selling John's car; visions of sales like the smoke could have been intoxicating.

Likely a lot of business decisions were made at that first showing. The agreement to go into business had already been made,
so details of how to go about it were likely quick to lay out. John
would have seen his machine handled by the others, as they all
became convinced of the vehicle's reliability and comfort. The car
was a reality and John had created it. Al was practical enough to
see a unique product for market, for he immediately put his experienced salesmanship to work for it.

Jim Swoveland, the teenage son of the village druggist where
John bought his gasoline, must have given John an admiring eye
and asked just the right questions, for he had been allowed into
the room where John worked on putting together the automobile
while others were not. Young Jim joined the Lambert men for
the covert runs. When the sun went down and the villagers were
allegedly in bed, thinking the cover of darkness kept their secret,
John and his intimates took the buggy out onto the streets of
Enterprise. But surely neighbors peeked out their windows and
rumors must have been flying. Back then some folks claimed it
was God's Will people travel by horse and John must have been
reviled as going against His Purpose. But the young inventor was
undeterred. Stories of those moonlit rides have come down to the
present day. They describe John taking his car and his friends outside of town onto the frozen fields of consenting farmers to open
up his ride on the relatively flat surface of the wintering land.
Imagine their thoughts as they rode. The car could speed up to
fifteen miles-per-hour. It must have felt like flying! To move over
the ground free from the view of a horse's tail must have been
liberating, if not outright disorienting. With the cold air of the
clear winter nights biting their cheeks, they took turns driving the
peppy little car which showed its worth as it successfully covered
ground.

John no doubt fed his own lust for speed but he was also pushing his product to look for ways to make it run better. The single
front wheel was not a good steering mechanism. He added springs
to soften the impact on the wheel; it did not help much. He then

added the steel tiller stick so the driver could rotate between using his hands and feet to steer, as one or the other became fatigued. As Ray notes, "John never again designed an automobile with a single front wheel." This assertion gives evidence to the theory that the entire Original Car did not burn, for tales of a John Lambert three-wheeled car emerge in 1895.

The Lamberts of Union worked with John on the promotion plan. This item posed a unique challenge; no one had heard of a gasoline-powered carriage for sale. But the Lamberts were skilled at describing their products in ads and their name carried a good reputation. Al and John drew up a list for a mailing. The Lamberts were hopeful; the promotional letter was sent out. I tried to find one of these original promotional letters; I wrote dozens of libraries and museums in my quest but in the end was unsuccessful. Could one of these letters be harbored in a setting I didn't contact? I'm thinking Al and John's list included a wide spectrum of possible purchasers whose descendants or hometown historians might still be able to put their hands on a copy.

After the mailing was done advertising the motorized buggy John had some time to bounce around in his little prototype with its stylish spindle seat and graceful large back wheels. It was a source of fascination and pleasure. Reports say he would take it out to the farmer's fields and along the unpaved, primitive roads of the time. Although in the future the first car owners would "house" their cars for the winter, John took advantage of the frozen ground to run his invention. By himself, John must have traveled hard with the wind and precipitation in his face. The rides must have been like a long drink to a thirsty man. As well I bet he ran into mechanical difficulties on many a trip. Ray states he remembers riding in this first car. I wish he had elaborated but he would have been only three. It was an anomaly in a world of horses and mules and no doubt attracted many a curious onlooker and would-be mechanic. John must have been enchanted by what he had created.

In the warmer months of 1891 John offered rides to his neighbors in Enterprise. Many have in more recent years written out affidavits describing their experiences as witnesses to and passengers in John's amazing buggy. In his eighties, Mr. Swoveland signed an affidavit testifying to his experiences. This document, held by the Smithsonian Institution, is a major piece of evidence that establishes the fact of John's priority. Mr. Swoveland attended the ceremonies in 1968 in Ohio City dedicating the historical markers for the factory and John's house. He is pictured with my dad and my dad's cousin John Lee on the front page of the Van Wert *Times Bulletin*.

The Anderson *Herald* ran an article about these testimonies. One witness to the three-wheeled buggy of 1891 remembered thinking, "Where in heaven's name is the horse?" Another recalls how, as teenage boys, they were excited to see the horseless carriage cough and belch as it idled and they were permitted to examine it close up. Another witness attested she watched with enchantment as her father sat next to John Lambert on the fancy leather seat of the three-wheeled carriage as it peppered through the village. Charles Koogle owned a farm close to town. Telling about the times John drove the car out to their farm to get eggs, Mr. Koogle said John "churned up the dust" as he drove away.

On one such early outing, with Jim Swoveland perched at his side, John was driving the buggy into the center of the village when the vehicle hit a root stump from a nearby tree sticking up out of the surface of the packed dirt street and veered the single front wheel into a hitching rack for horses at the side of the road. No one was hurt including the car. A group of nearby men helped pull the car backward, for there was no provision for reverse. With the direction corrected, the car continued on its way. This first automobile accident on United States soil, which happened in 1891, is commemorated with a sign, "First Auto Wreck," at the original location in Enterprise (now Ohio City), Van Wert County, Ohio.

The car John Lambert operated in 1891 was a mechanical success but it did not sell. As it was, the promotional letters John and Al sent out did not attract even that one order. Had there been one order, the Lamberts would have filled it and Lambert car production would have officially begun. Thereafter John would have openly promoted the status of being The First and historians would be clear on the fact. The Lamberts received a number of inquiries in response to their letter, some about the vehicle and some about the engine, but not one inquiry led to a sale. I am very interested in these letters of response because by my logic they should still be in the family collection but are not. Certainly John and his brothers, Ray, John Lee, my Dad, or any of those who had been in a position to salvage items of the era would have treasured any and all of the responses to their first promotional letter for an automobile, yet none exist in any family file. Ray specifically refers to them in the four pages of questions and lists several of the names of the senders, so I believe he did have them in his possession up to a certain point. And now they're missing. Isn't it reasonable to suspect they were among the items in the legendary lost briefcase?

Sadly, the original car does not exist today. Many sources ascribe its loss to the implement store fire in Enterprise in late 1891, but other sources describe a three-wheeled automobile as existing after that date. Perhaps due to the distractions of other projects and numerous relocations or the need to claim pieces to use on new experiments, it was lost in stages. Information pertaining to the physical appearance of the Original Car is limited to several items in addition to word descriptions: a drawing by draftsman Mr. Wacholtz, another drawing by John and of course the professional photograph taken by Walter Lewis in Enterprise for $1.25 in August of 1891, a good price for an important piece of American history. The photograph is a crisp portrait showing fine detail. What we see looks light enough to bounce off the crown of the muddy ruts of the streets around town and almost too light to take on the sturdy beasts that ruled the roads of the time. Artists have since recreated the image of John's car, notably the murals in Ohio City and in Winchester, Indiana, and the color plates published in books like Clarence P. Hornung's *Portrait Gallery of Early Automobiles*. I have seen one miniature restoration that is privately owned. Built by Anderson, Indiana and John Lambert historian Dan Davis in 1995, with the help of his wife Barb, it is 12.5 inches high. Like the original it is very light. Barb fashioned the leather upholstery including tiny little covered buttons, just like the original; Dan did everything else. He knew the back wheels had to be right and created them first. He built a little replica motor and included little foot pedals and a thin tiller stick. The driver's cushion lifts out for access to the receiving tank. Dan took his miniature Lambert to his lectures about Anderson history including his favorite topic John Lambert and to countless antique engine and auto meets. My dad beamed ear to ear when he saw it and was able to take it into his hands and see its details. The wheels turn, the engine rolls but it does not run. It holds very close to descriptions of the original and is a one-to-six scale.

Chapter 5

The Buckeye Gasoline Engine

Being practical men, the Lambert entrepreneurs immediately saw promise in developing and manufacturing John's compact gasoline engine. They believed the public was ready to replace their cumbersome steam engines for the manageability of a gasoline model. A small market was established already in the boating industry, a tiny niche compared to the open possibilities. John's gasoline engines could be pulled through crop fields to run threshers, tillers, cutters, cultivators, reapers, mowers, planters, binders and loaders. They could be sold to run fans and electric lights, ovens, presses, and water pumps. They would supplement the strength of workers to lift and haul loads and run construction machinery. At the urging of his relatives who envisioned farmers and businessmen eager for an energy source small enough to drag to different locations, John decided to give this endeavor his full attention. It was a momentous decision but not difficult to make. He was confident he could design the model and agreed the prospects looked lucrative. He sold all his holdings in Enterprise as he prepared to move his family to Union City. He left the home he established on his own in Van Wert County, Ohio and returned to the heart of his family's enterprise in Union, Darke County, Ohio. He assumed the title of President of the newly named Buckeye Manufacturing Company, the company he created with his father and two brothers to produce his gasoline engines. George and Al set up production space to manufacture John's engine in their Union facilities previously occupied by the Pioneer Pole and Shaft Company, a longtime partner. The Pioneer Pole and Shaft Company, whose flagship site was Sydney, Ohio, was moving to new, larger facilities in Anderson, Indiana.

John Lambert was pioneering Gottlieb Otto's four-stroke gasoline engine, the European precursor to our present-day gasoline engines. In 1890, with his horseless carriage in mind, he had partnered with John Hicks of Cleveland to work on one of America's first gasoline engines. John's engine was possibly the first to be developed in this country for use in individual cars. Hicks had acquired the European patent with plans to convert a stationery engine to motorize tramway cars. By agreeing that the engine he intended to develop would not be used for either railway or tramcars, John began development of his engine. With a two hundred dollar investment John sent instructions to one of Hicks' engineers, Mr. William Wacholtz in Cleveland, to work on his version of the three-cylinder prototype. Mr. Wacholtz could not get it to run so John had the engine sent to him to nearby Van Wert where in a short period of time he had the engine running. His one-cylinder version went quite beyond what Hicks had offered and was indeed strong enough to move his buggy.

Because the complete car was not a viable product John went back to his work shed and designed what he believed to be a unique, practical stationary engine that his family could put into production. He gained patent protection for his complete system in 1893. (picture of patent) Soon the Lamberts were in business with a 2-cylinder, 12-pound standing model gasoline engine they called the Buckeye.

To use an analogy, this was John offering America its first alcoholic drink. America went wild, going on a 100-year bender and is only now sobering up.

Buckeye engine sales were brisk almost immediately as farmers and industrialists alike stepped forward to implement the new energy source into their work routines. Like sea captains and boat enthusiasts before them, they turned away from their old steam engines with their need for coal and their dangerous fires for a new engine run by portable fuel. An embossed label on the machine itself displayed the list of patents that backed up Lambert family claims to selling the best power source of the age.

Engine production probably began in earnest in late 1892 or early 1893. There are differing dates ranging from 1889-1894. Perhaps the 1889 date was given as the very beginning of John's work on a gasoline engine for any purpose. And then perhaps output was achieved in stages. Most likely because of the highly competitive marketplace and in order to guard against the prevalence of copycats, the finished units were stored and actual shipment was postponed while the patents were pending. John writes to Ray he "began in the gasoline engine business in the fall of 1892." My best guess is that the brothers began organizing their engine production late in 1891 with John building the prototype and the Union men tooling the factory. At the same time Minnie was packing up to leave Enterprise, John collected his patents. I imagine John commuted down to Union on a regular basis for only he knew how to set up the workstations in the manufacturing plant and specify their supplies. The Union company had suffered a fire in spring of 1891 and was already rebuilt when the factory was again redesigned in the fall in preparation for the Buckeye.

The Buckeye Manufacturing Company was organized with John as President. "Buckeye" was the name given to the latest Lambert Big Hit. This Ohio family used the name of the spherical lucky pieces from the buckeye tree so plentiful in their home state for their product, the Buckeye. How exciting the launch must have been! I wish I could have toured The Buckeye Manufacturing Company when the site was running at full production, smelled the oil and fire in the air, seen the foundry, heard the sounds of the tools and the voices of the workers as they produced these engines, if not the first among the very first gasoline engines to be produced in America. When the patent approvals arrived, had I been there I bet I would have seen the boys in a mad dash to send out orders and collect their profits. Like so many Americans they scurried to get their invention to market because they wanted to make a lot of money.

John's little powerhouse proved to be very popular. Al was keen to watch the numbers as sales skyrocketed. Orders soon overran their manufacturing capacity and before the end of 1893, within only months of their original output, they decided to expand to new facilities. They wanted to take advantage of the immediate demand. The brothers did their research among locations and like the Pioneer Pole and Shaft Company chose to open their new plant forty miles away in Anderson, Indiana for its favorable location on and near rich fields of natural gas. It so happens that the very first person I met when I moved to Boston, Massachusetts as a twenty-two year old was another young woman Melody who was originally from a tiny farm town down the road from Anderson. We were both amazed at the rural Indiana link from our pasts. The Lambert brothers found Anderson well served by four rail lines and well fueled by a seemingly endless supply of natural gas. (That supply began to run out in 1912, a mere twenty-five years later and is now long gone.) The city leaders in Anderson offered a better deal to the young brothers than options offered in Union, Indiana or anywhere in Ohio. The Lamberts had a large brick factory space constructed on Second and Sycamore Street. Late in 1893 in accordance with their expansion plans, John established the Lambert Gas and Gasoline Engine Company and moved his family to Anderson, as did many of his siblings and his parents. Production was interdependent between the two locations. Parts made in Ohio were shipped for assembly in Indiana. A few years later, the first Lambert-made automobile models were completed in Union, but their engines were manufactured in Anderson. The two sites had easy railroad linkage through Muncie and Winchester in Indiana.

Although most of the family now lived in Indiana, John's older brother Al continued to live in Ohio with his wife Eva and their children. Their house which Al had built in 1884 is still along the main road outside Union; today it is restored and listed on the National Registry of Historical Places as an example of Italianate style architecture with its ten-foot ceilings, sliding wall doors and slated roof and an original stained-glass window. Al, in addition to his association with Buckeye, helped run the Union Granary. He served on the Board of Otterbein College in Ohio where he gave an entire building in his wife's name. After many years of use, it was lost to fire.

Even without gasoline in the mix, fire was an ever-present threat to all citizens of the era, urban and rural, including the industrialists, businessmen and farmers forging the economy of the industrial revolution. In a world before plastic, safety standards and extensive fireproofing, fast moving fire was a real danger. Most houses and commercial buildings were made of wood, including most contents as well. Everything was flammable. Back in John's day everyone had a close connection with fire and so every one understood its terror. Although never the direct victim, on three occasions I have watched fire fighters battling blazes mere yards from where I lived. Admiration burned in my chest with the heat of what I witnessed. I think of Minnie's perspective as she watched her husband go off to work on his experiments and I wonder not if, but how vociferous were her warnings and objections. And I wonder how she reacted to gasoline becoming a centerpiece of the Lambert enterprise. She knew fire was a danger; it happened often enough to others. The Lamberts were not immune and over the years lost a considerable amount of commercial property and forward momentum to the smoke and flames of accidental blazes.

Newspaper accounts at the time tell of a Saturday, April 25, 1891 fire that completely destroyed John's granary silo in Enterprise, which he rebuilt before selling it on his way out of town the following year. The "alert" for this fire (or "alarm") was sent by telegraph to Van Wert, Ohio at 5 pm. Their help was thirty minutes away, a different standard than today. It is little wonder the silo was a complete loss. Reports say the fire started in the engine room. Another fire in October of the same year burned John's implement store. This fire is blamed for the loss of the original car prototype. The cause of this fire, as reported through word of mouth over the decades and originating from Minnie, was from a lantern igniting natural gas fumes. Her issuance of this report must have set her teeth on edge, no matter the cause. John did indeed play with sparks and gasoline. John's interest was in what leapt between the two; his success was in harnessing it and putting it to work.

During his Enterprise years John suffered another devastating blaze, this one in his lumberyard. The flames took his entire inventory of freshly milled wood and at the time it looked like he was ruined. A lumberman in Dayton heard about John's bad luck and, unbeckoned, sent a truck loaded with lumber to put my great grandfather back in business. John eventually paid back the generous man but his timely action saved the business. My dad reports John and then Ray carried affection throughout their lives for the man who sent the lumber, a Peter Kuhns who ran a large lumberyard south of Dayton. A friend of mine from Dayton, Katherine Kuhns, who lives close to me here in Massachusetts, is related to that Peter Kuhns. Our parents were friends as we grew up. Here she and I are three generations later, enjoying our mutual deep-seeded connections.

In May of 1892 the entire Main Street of Enterprise went up in smoke and flames. Most of the business district had to be replaced. A fire after a severe storm in Sydney, Ohio destroyed the Pioneer Pole and Shaft Company's main plant and necessitated their complete move to Anderson in 1906. As earlier noted, fire ravaged the Union City factory in 1891, taking $15,000 in inventory and destroying the building just before they began manufacturing John's stationery engine. Fire plagued other automobile pioneers; the second place winner of the 1895 Chicago *Herald* road race was killed in a fiery explosion as he worked on another prototype in 1896. A devastating fire through his workspace took all Ran Olds had in 1899 except for one model, which he put into production. That car became America's first popular car, the Curved Dash Wonder. In more modern times (1969) the old Lambert factory building in Anderson burned. A photographer at the scene got spectacular pictures of the blaze. The Lambert venture after World War One to build tractors in California failed and one story of its end was that fire played a role.

From the time the Lamberts first moved to Anderson they were in business with the Howe Fire Apparatus Company. One source said Howe moved to Anderson to be near the Buckeye MC and that the Lamberts supplied all their chassis. Along with their personal experiences perhaps the great devastation of the Chicago fire in 1871 helped inspire the Lambert brothers to consider fire-fighting technology. It inspired many innovative Americans of that generation to develop better systems to fight and prevent fire. The fire fighting tools folks back then confronted were crude and inefficient by today's standards. The bucket line, horse-drawn or hand-propelled wagons, and hand pumped water were the order of the day, but were soon to be upgraded with motorized wagons carrying motorized pumps. The Chicago fire, which destroyed 17,000 buildings, literally devastating the city, was fought with the help of steam power; steam engine pressure pushed water through hoses carried by hand or horse propelled trucks. The 1906 fire after the San Francisco earthquake was fought largely with the ancient method of bucket brigade. The first truck to be propelled and water to be pumped by the same engine was used in 1907. San Francisco did not abandon their horse-drawn steam engine wagons until 1922. Certainly the science of fire fighting interested the early Lamberts, for they produced fire equipment throughout their manufacturing history before and after automobile production. During World War One, the Lamberts partnered with Howe and Ford to build fire trucks for the United States War Department.

From the beginning, as chief engineer of their product, John dictated the specifics of manufacture of the Buckeye gasoline engine. Throughout the 1890's he continued to design improvements and he accrued more patents for his innovations. By 1895 he had three complete systems under patent protection. The *Muncie Evening Press'* headline for John Lambert's obituary names him "Holder of First Patent for Gas Engines".

Today, there exist only a few of those early Buckeye gasoline engines. They are truly historic in their own right, even with no automobile surrounding it. It is no wonder to me the large number of individuals around the world who are infatuated with antique engines. I certainly caught the bug. I have experienced a Buckeye running with my own eyes and ears and viewed pictures of other Buckeye models. They are beautiful. As my friends ran their graceful machine for me in their backyard, Dan and Barb Davis exuded a warm, palpable pride in their Buckeye. I have contacted a number of antique engine organizations and talked to enthusiasts who cheerfully invited me, the social worker and no gearhead, to their shows and museums. Is there something about those old machines that breeds a sharing kind of affection? I have heard of exaggerators and liars in their midst but of no one not charmed by the syncopation and graceful maneuverings of those very early power-generating machines.

It was during this time that John began concentrating on a technology that would bring him national fame and shows his mind was on automobile technology during this period. It is an idea that is still admired and in use today. He began developing his friction drive transmission. The concept is simple, a John Lambert signature quality. He designed a sophisticated system of acceleration involving two perpendicular metal disks that made contact on a line of friction. As one disk slid along the other, the engine accelerated; when that disk passed the meridian of the other, the engine entered the reverse gear. A patented plate made of layers of paper used between the two disks had to be replaced periodically at a whopping cost of twenty-five cents. Except for this minor maintenance, the method was durable and strong. All Lambert cars produced for sale to the public over the years with a few exceptions used this method of transmission. Those who drove these cars swore by the performance. Demonstrations of rigorous tests on Lambert cars showed the power of this system. Across the street from the factory in Union the Lamberts constructed a monstrous wooden incline that looks in part like a roller coaster ride. Here they could conveniently demonstrate the reliable power of their system. John himself liked to be the driver. He ran his cars up the steps of public buildings, pulled loads up numerous steep manmade inclines and competed in punishing races. Scores of testimonial letters are included in Lambert promotional brochures of which quite a few exist today that display the Lambert awards and proclaim customer satisfaction with their friction drive Lambert cars. John's patents for this gearless system grew in number and eventually this work would bring him the title *Father of the Gradual Transmission*.

This transmission was fully developed and in place for John's first commercially viable car. These first models, called Unions, were equipped with the dual plates of the unique power transmission. It was called the car with one thousand speeds and in fact provided a smooth, one-gear acceleration or upon breaking a steady decline in speed.

Chapter 6

The Stage is Set

Throughout the successful run of the Buckeye, John indeed did not give up on the idea of a commercially viable self-propelled car. He and his family enjoyed the financial prosperity gotten from his gasoline engine business. In 1899 the Lamberts had their large home on Hendricks Street built. While John traveled around the country on engine business. I saw letters from Minnesota and Wisconsin and a travel expense log from a trip to New York City and Boston that cost him $69.12. Minnie stayed in Anderson and oversaw the construction and outfitting of their home. As the years of the 1890's passed John remained convinced that the day of the horseless carriage was coming and he stayed involved. He considered its eventual appeal to be convenience and luxury. His assumption was that traveling professional men like his father-in-law the doctor, businessmen and men of means would be the first customers. He watched developments in Europe; he saw public interest flicker in America and he waited for a flame. The premiere issue of *Horseless Carriage*, an American publication, came out in November 1893, before any American outfit manufactured an automobile for market. It was widely read. People were getting interested. Reports in the magazine described the commercial possibilities among the experimental vehicles of the day, which included a project by John Lambert. The publication printed a picture of John's original 1891 three-wheeled car as a current proposed commercial venture along with an article that described my great-grandfather's intentions to put his self-propelled gasoline-powered vehicle into production. John must have had pieces of the old vehicle, which he would need in case he did get inquiries or orders. John dropped his hook into commercial waters once again, but still there was no nibble. Although he did not strike on commercial success this time either, John's tinkering continued.

Of all the automotive pioneers, Elwood Haynes was closest to my great-grandfather. I think Elwood was a familiar figure around the John Lambert household of Anderson, Indiana from the time the family moved there. John and Elwood's friendship dated back even further than Anderson, to when John still lived in Ohio, for Elwood had served as field supervisor in Jay County when he helped to found the Indiana Gas Company which was adjacent to Union City. At the time they bought farmland together in Jay County. Elwood had gone East for his education. After graduating from Worcester Polytechnic Institute in Massachusetts, he did graduate work at John Hopkins. Between, he was a teacher and school principal back in Indiana and after, he managed the gas fields. A curious and innovative man, he had a special interest in metallurgy, the study of metals. He married his wife Bertha who urged him to invent tableware that did not need polishing. He would later invent stainless steel.

John and Elwood had much in common from the start with their curious and prolific minds. Both were one of ten children born within three years of each other and raised in Midwestern homes with prominent fathers, one a judge, the other, a manufacturer. Both were Presbyterians. Before the bond of inventive inclination, John and Elwood's mutual interests, according to reports in my family, cemented a friendship of admiration and enjoyment. They offered each other strengths in separate talents upon which to sharpen their wits. Of the two men, perhaps one was awed by the formal education of the other while the other was perhaps a touch jealous of the other's mechanical ability. These differences were also likely sources of respect and an inspiring competition. In 1893 Elwood lived in Kokomo, Indiana, fifty miles from Anderson towards Chicago.

Elwood and John were to become members of a larger salon of automotive pioneers who lived and worked in and around Indiana that included such famous names as the founder of Chrysler, William C. Durant, the three Chevrolet brothers, John and Horace Dodge, Jonathan Maxwell, head of GM, as well as others and local, lesser known entrepreneurs, mechanics and engineers. Indiana was to become the first American hub of automotive manufacture. At one point, by one count, there were two hundred outfits producing vehicles for sale, more by far than any other state. Although there are no records of attendees, it is documented that John and Minnie regularly entertained kindred spirits of the burgeoning industry. Minnie had a culinary reputation of capably orchestrating delicious and comfortable meals. The guest lists included those just mentioned and others as well. The content of what had to be lively conversations I can only fantasize about. Imagine Will Durant sitting with Louis Chevrolet visualizing a new car company over coffee or brandy! John may have heard confidential musings from his friends the Dodge Brothers for they were in an argument with Henry Ford in Detroit, or about Henry Leland's designs for his ultimate luxury car; he designed both the Cadillac and the Lincoln. Maybe Leland's persnicketiness for accuracy gained conviction after talking with these other master machinists, for he developed interchangeable parts, an important factor in Ford's future success. John Maxwell, who built a car that became a Chrysler, was a friend of the Lamberts. Many, many sources describe the Lambert household as a popular setting beginning before the century turned and lasting long into the next. The big Lambert house on Hendricks Street in Anderson is still an elegant setting with its double parlors and sun-drenched dining room.

In 1893, as John was experiencing a rush of success selling his newly introduced gasoline engines, perhaps motivated by the articles in *Horseless Carriage*, perhaps in the intimate setting of the Haynes or the Lambert dining room, Elwood told John he was working on plans to put a gas-propelled vehicle on the market, that he had recently made the acquaintance of two brothers in Kokomo, Elmer and Edgar Apperson who ran the Riverside Repair Shop, and he believed they had the mechanical aptitude to build to his specifications. John knew the long careful process he had walked through to come up with his own design. Even then, he ran into numerous practical problems. When Elwood talked about using a Sintz upright stationary marine engine, John saw the content of Elwood's plan, in that it was like the Duryeas' in Massachusetts: Elwood was going to use an existing engine. He would install someone else's motor into his vehicle and then concoct the transmission. John's project was different; his car including all of its parts had been designed by him expressly for the purpose they served. I am guessing this difference had significance to John. Not being built to carry the weight of the engine, the horse carriage thus converted had problems with maneuverability and accommodating the engine's vibrations. John was tackling engineering challenges his friend was likely to overlook. Believing his ideas were unique, there would be less competitive inclination. Elwood announced he wanted to advertize his product nationally as "America's First Automobile" and he asked John not to contradict him. John agreed. Understandably in some sources today Elwood Haynes is named as the builder of America's first car; but he was not.

Quickly after Elwood, with the Apperson brothers, went into production, so did the Duryea brothers in far away Massachusetts. Elwood advertized his Haynes automobiles as "America's First Car" and continued to do so throughout his long career manufacturing automobiles, which lasted into the '20's; he died in 1925. The Duryeas thought they were first to go to market with a horseless carriage. Their production lasted three years at which time Frank joined a new partner to produce the Stevens-Duryea. That enterprise also lasted into the 1920's.

The Duryeas, originally from Peoria, Illinois and with ties there, took a four-wheeled horse buggy and combined with a single-cylinder, four horse power gasoline engine that they ran down Spruce Street in Springfield, Massachusetts on September 20, 1893. Elwood, on the other hand or more to the point on the other side of the Appalachians, rode his prototype on the Pumpkinvine Pike, a country road near Kokomo, Indiana on July 4, 1894. Any Midwesterner, as I originally was, knows that home feels like the center of the universe and Massachusetts is a long way away. I have been a Massachusetts resident for my adult life and have learned the natives here see their region as "The Start of It All." I can imagine that back in 1894, before telephones and airplanes, television or the Internet, it came as a shock to both camps to hear of the other. Meanwhile, the man who actually did build America's first automobile all by himself was working in his shed, coming up with new ideas – the bumper! – to make things better. As his daughter Mae said in the 1969 newspaper article, "Father was more interested in inventing than he was in making himself famous."

The Duryeas's claim of being the inventors of America's first automobile is still cited in some sources; it is not true. They were the first to go into production with a gasoline-powered car but were not the inventors of America's First Car. John writes, in response to one of Ray's questions, that the Duryeas never claimed to have made the first car because one brother Charles had traveled to Ohio City and "found I had built it." (Hey, wait, here is John saying *I built the first car*.... Ray asks: "Did Chas. Duryea ever make claims as to having built the first automobile in America prior to recent years?" and John answers, "not to my knowledge. He went to Ohio City and found I had built it." Sounds to me like John says here, "I built the first car." Ray then asks, "It seems to me that Elwood Haynes made these claims, and that you permitted him to make them because of some certain specific friendship or because of the fact that you felt you were doing him a business and personal favor. As I remember it, the battle used to be between Ackerson (sic) and Haynes as to who built the first car, they both having worked on it together, according to my memory." John does not answer the comments, but corrects Ackerson for Apperson, and Ray goes on to another subject.) History books describe the feud over who should claim credit for the priority moniker between Elwood and his mechanics; likewise the bitter well-documented battle over the same issues divided the two Duryea brothers. How can I blame John for staying out of the mess?

John let others do the math. Although he often referred to his 1891 prototype, he never wavered in his silence on the matter of priority for the remaining fifty-nine years of his life. From my point of reference, this promise was like Prince Edward abdicating the British throne. Who would give away this rightfully held moniker? Who could sit back and be quiet while the question of who built America's first car was often discussed? The debate over whose car was first grew loud at times but the actual builder kept quiet. On the other hand, John did not stop his son from accumulating evidence that documents his premiere achievement and in fact participated to help gather affidavits from old Ohio City neighbors who had witnessed that first historic car. Scott Bailey, esteemed auto historian, pointed out in an email to me, "The key piece of evidence of course is the sworn statement given by Walter Lewis dated and sworn to in 1927." Along with the other neighbors' statements, the Jim Swoveland affidavit and the photograph by Walter Lewis, the evidence adds up.

As a businessman, John saw commerce as a grand game. He called it a game in an answer to one of Ray's questions. The field of the game was the marketplace and John's original car did not succeed there. Elwood was now planning his try at selling a self-propelled, gasoline-fueled vehicle. From the perspective of 1893, when the request was made, there may have been logic to production of Elwood's automobiles being "The First". It depends on your definition of "first". First car to be built was John's; first car to sell would be Elwood's (or rather, the Duryea's). John did not act with an eye on his place in history. He did honor his friendship with Elwood. The historic legacy of his primary invention his great-grandchildren would inherit was not his motivation. If I were to ask John today why he let Elwood walk away with the title of building America's first car, he would explain to me that Elwood had stock holders while he, John, with the backing of his family, had no moneylenders to please.

I don't want to diminish the pioneering genius of the Duryeas or John's friend Elwood Haynes or any other claimants, only their claim on priority. Because evidence indicates John was riding in his car in January, 1891, it is likely safe to disregard other 1891 claimants. I bet there were dozens of tinkerers applying themselves to the task of a horseless carriage, most of whom are lost to history. For discussion I settle for those for whom there is documentation. Henry Nadig worked in Allentown, Pennsylvania; Charles Black in Indianapolis; Gottfried Schloemer and Frank Toepfer were in Milwaukee, Wisconsin. Their claims are not backed with the strong evidence that supports the date of John's vehicle. But all these accomplishments happened so quickly from our frame of time that it seems the inventors worked together. Although in some cases only months apart, under close and extensive research as the Editor of *Antique Automobile*, L. Scott Bailey pinpointed the initial date of each of their vehicles as running after John's. They all deserve our admiration and study. When an idea's time has come, it often appears in several locations at once or nearly at once. By 1900 the time for the ottomobile had arrived. Nine years prior John Lambert first put a gas-powered car on the road. There are still some who claim the wrong man; I want to set the record straight. Henry Ford, remember, is famous for popularizing the automobile by devising the moving assembly line. He mass produced cars, not just for the elite, but for everyone; he did not invent the automobile.

Sometime early in the 1920's Charles Duryea made a visit to the Smithsonian Museum in Washington DC. There he saw Elwood Haynes 1894 car displayed with a prominent sign labeling it "America's First Gasoline Powered Vehicle." Mr. Duryea was easily roused anyway and this roused him considerably. He knew his vehicle predated the Haynes. Upset with officials of the Smithsonian he nonetheless presented them with his 1893 vehicle. Both historic vehicles are now at the Smithsonian. How marvelous that they still exist; how I wish John's pretty little buggy could be displayed beside them! Remnants of Henry Nadig's vehicle were in more recent times the basis of a modified restoration. Its first run was later in the year 1891. Charles Black of Indianapolis, so close to John in Anderson, completed his Benz-inspired four-wheeled car in 1893 by placing a gasoline engine in an ordinary buggy. It is now at the Indianapolis Children's Museum. Also available for viewing in the Milwaukee Public Museum is the Schloemer-Toepfer 1892 vehicle. The two men reportedly sat over a bucket of beer (the method of its distribution in those days), talking and sketching to devise their prototype. They used a Sintz engine.

Later in the 1920's Charles Duryea made a visit to Ohio City to investigate what he had heard about the priority of the John Lambert vehicle. I guess this was when he said, "Yes, John Lambert built the first gasoline-powered car." His visit was mentioned in the *Ohio City Progress*, a weekly newspaper, in an April 1, 1927 article that featured John Lambert's visit to town that Scott Bailey cites. John was with Ray to collect affidavits and statements. The paper listed fifty-one living residents who were witness to John's 1891 car. My best guess is that this was the occasion that Ray collected and lost affidavits signed by other men of the industry who gathered for the visit, which stated John Lambert's prototype predated any of the others. Dad said Ray had a briefcase for the meeting in Ohio City and collected signatures designating John's priority. These missing affidavits have been described by several sources. Questions of theft have been handled discreetly and gently by all in my family. Whatever happened, it is lost to history.

I can't help but wonder what Ray might have been carrying. The depth of his loss may have been deep indeed. The four-page list of questions that Ray wrote for his father to answer was so respectful and gentle compared to the frustration he must have felt. On one question to his father, Ray lists by name several of the writers of the 1891 letters requesting more information on John's original prototype. He was trying to cajole his father's recollections but John let the question stand. That leaves me the names but no letters. The actual letters may have been in the briefcase that was stolen or lost on Ray's return from Ohio City. They would be valuable evidence in the case for John's priority status. Ray described them as "still existing" but I have not found them. One, Ray writes, is dated early February 1891 and so sets a very early outside date for the completion of John's vehicle and the initial road test. Ray worked hard to establish the fact of John's priority and John cooperated. It does not matter, really, that so much was lost. Ray's efforts were rewarded. Once Scott Bailey's article appeared in *Antique Automobile* John's place was established. Most writings since that article acknowledge John's priority.

I draw conclusions about John's character based on what I call the Elwood-angle. Although I deeply admire John for his inventive and entrepreneurial genius, I admire him also for keeping his word. It was obviously important to him. Was he ever tempted, in the years to follow, to claim his rightful place as The First? For example, during the years his own company battled in the marketplace to sell Lambert automobiles or later after World War One and Lambert car production had ceased? Even after Elwood's death John allowed the story to stand. The personality his grandson, my father, describes was one of quiet confidence, a "sweetheart" and "a genius". I really don't think he cared about the title, the credit or posterity. I bet he saw the advantage of staying out of it. His giant inventive intellect occupied his time within the context of a large, functioning landed family, the one he grew up in and the one he and Minnie created. No family is perfect and tales of Lambert failures and shenanigans are told in this book.

Nonetheless, in his life John was surrounded by a situation that reflected back to him his successes in business, in his community and in his relationships. He never suffered an outcast's insecurities; he lived his life with a sense of belonging. With other of his horns blaring he didn't need to toot this one. By the end of his life, I can't help but recall, he held over six hundred patents.

Chapter 7

The Lambert Automobile Company

My Dad smiled a lot when he told me of a particular time his grandfather had driven over to Dayton to fetch him for a stay in Anderson in about 1928. He must have been a boy of only five or six, for he was born after the family's car manufacturing days but still early in car history. Young Billy was going to the big stately house on Hendricks Street for a visit with his grandparents and to spend time with the large group of Lambert and Kelley relatives living in Anderson. The Hendricks Street home always sheltered extended family during John and Minnie's occupancy. As well, the car magnate had had three small "bungalows" (they look like one-bedroom, single-story homes) built on a street within view of his front door. These and other houses were occupied with relatives, Emma and her children, the Longneckers, younger brothers and their families, and of course Mae and her family including my dad's childhood playmate, cousin John Lee. John had a much younger sister named Jennifer. On that trip to Dayton, my great-grandfather could have been driving a Haynes or an Apperson; over the years he had received gifts of each from his friends in Kokomo. Which ever it was, I am sure it was a large and luxurious model. The last Lamberts had been manufactured in 1917.

For the trip John took Route 40 which used to be the National Highway bringing pioneers to the new West and was now piloted by Model A's, Packard Super 8's and Nashes. With the youngster next to him, the old car builder drove back toward Anderson across the rich farmlands of the central Midwest. When they were almost to their destination John turned to his grandson out of the blue and announced he wanted to make a stop. "Billy," my dad quoted, "I hope you won't mind. I have to look for my glasses." They had been passing miles of cleared crop fields and were now between two fields with no house or intersection in sight. John slowed the car and drove off to the side of the road. Dad recalled his amazement at seeing his Grandfather leave him on the front seat, get out of the car and walk through a hole in a farmer's fence onto the cleared ground of an adjacent field. Billy watched as his grandfather scanned the site, walked a bit and then bent to pick up something that glinted in the sun. John fixed his glasses onto his face. He had lost, gone back and miraculously found his eyeglasses. My dad laughed as he supposed how those glasses came to rest among the stubble in the field. To be sure I was understanding correctly, I asked my Dad to explain, which he did in a conspiratorial tone, "I imagine once he was out on his own he had stopped to do a little sport-driving." My great-grandfather was known to have assessed his own models with grueling tests on open fields. As a young man he was attracted by speed and pushing vehicular performance; he apparently continued his interest in driving fast into his grandfatherly years. Back in his day, either alone or with a fellow enthusiast, John had the habit of going out onto the fields of neighboring farmers where he could open up the engine to its top performance. Apparently the sixty-eight-year old had detoured on his ride to Dayton for a little "sport-driving" on the open field all by himself and during the wild ride he lost his glasses when they had been jarred from his nose.

Dan Davis of Anderson told another story of one such sport-driving adventure that explains how John came to wear a mustache. While out on a field behind the wheel of one of his models,

John drove through an unanticipated barbed wire fence. It ripped at his face and left a nasty cut on his upper lip. Lucky for John his wife was out of town attending a sick relative so she was not there to say, "I told you so." As the doctor was stitching him up in the Lambert kitchen, a messenger arrived to fetch the doctor. John's nephew Hugh had pulled a pot of boiling fruit jelly off the stove and was burned. Dr. Sears apologized to John as he finished with him quickly, the story goes, so he could rush to patch up young Hugh. The doctor tended both Lambert family members who had accidents one right after the other. Except in his senior years, ever after the accident, to hide the scar from his reckless ride John wore a mustache, which ironically flattered his appearance.

The first manufacturers of American automobiles understood the wildfire quality of the general public's interest in speed and danger. Driving fast quickly became a sport of interest to early car enthusiasts. Bicycle and horse racing were already popular spectator sports. It took very little time to rev up car racing popularity which worked hand-in-glove with selling automobiles. Breaking speed records became a popular pastime. Crowds formed from the beginning to watch the fearlessness of the drivers and the power of the new vehicles they operated for there was little control at their breakneck speeds. It gave mechanical engineers like John a chance to test their machines and was a birthing ground for new technologies. As the twentieth century opened, race car drivers like Barney Oldfield and Louis Chevrolet became like "rock stars" to the public with their speed and glorious recklessness and they became technical consultants to the automakers by offering suggestions and complaints to stimulate new ideas. My dad recalls stories that told of the early manufacturers themselves actually planning the races. This early community of auto pioneers had their sense of rivalry thwarted by their common mission to convince the public of the worthwhile nature of the automobile. In the rough and tumble beginning, to draw attention to their products and create a market, they would devise a racing course over existing roads or across a farmer's field and propose to compete.

They devised road races, hill climbs, reliability runs and long-distance trials. Recognizable racing events with prizes began with early races like the Gordon Bennett Cup and a year or so later, the Vanderbilt Cup; it was in the 1920's that race car design blossomed with such variety. The Indianapolis Speedway was first constructed in 1909. The time my dad speaks of was before the local oval tracks, which came in a rush after World War One.

This excuse to drive fast drew the spectators from the start. Dad said the company leaders perhaps would flip a coin to determine who would win. The object was to display their cars' performance. Folks gathered in large numbers, for the hometown-bound population was curious about what the new motorized buggies could do as well as being drawn to the daredevil nature of the event as drivers defied catastrophe by pushing the limits of their machines and their own skills. A dangerous pattern at road races emerged as spectators, like at parades, fanned out onto the empty street in order to catch the first glimpse of the on-coming cars. The racing vehicles would come up much more quickly than people expected or were able to move away from and in their rush to get out of the way numerous injuries and even a few deaths occurred. But for the most part these problems were controlled and the events were festive and exciting. By attending the events, Americans were being educated about the new technology. To further my alcohol/gasoline analogy, this era of racing recklessness was like a teen "kegger" in the woods. Gasoline-powered vehicles inflamed American greed for speed that has not been sated yet.

Even as the very first autos were constructed in Europe, the makers devised to display their cars and race them. Perhaps the world's first race of note was a 78-mile run from Paris to Rouen. Back then the "race" was more of a reliability test and the few vehicles that entered averaged the blazing speed of about twelve miles per hour. The buggies could achieve higher speeds, but tire trouble and mechanical difficulties brought down their averages and lengthened their time. The machines were crude, the roads were rough but the excitement was high. The next year, 1895, was the widely known Paris–Bordeaux race in Europe, an extensive distance of 732 miles won by a Peugeot.

Americans were quick to notice the excitement in Europe and planned a race on this side of the Atlantic. Chicago *Herald Tribune* editor Herman Kohlstaat organized a race for Thanksgiving Day, 1895. Response was so overwhelming President Cleveland ordered the War Department to oversee the event. Stories circulating in Anderson tell of John Lambert entering a three-wheeled buggy into the competition along with his friend Elwood Haynes who entered with his own buggy. Scott Bailey sites race entrant records that show John and Elwood each planned to enter a car in the race. They must have traveled the dusty highway up to Chicago together although I wonder about their confidence-levels even before they began. And indeed, both vehicles failed before they ever could start the race. The story I heard was that, with his car already sidelined, Elwood was behind the wheel of John's car with John in the rider's seat on the way to the starting line when one of the car's rear wheels ran up a telephone pole grounding wire. The car flipped and sustained damage beyond immediate repair leaving the two men to witness the race as spectators. There was up to a foot of freshly fallen snow on the ground that morning, so obstacles were covered, the going was slick and the air was bitter cold. Of eighty registrants, from a starting area plowed clear by a team of horses, only six cars began the fifty-five mile race to Evanston and back. Three were German-made Benz vehicles. Macy Department Store of Chicago sponsored one of the Benz with an eye to selling the imports in America. But the Benz were all defeated by the American-made machine of the Duryea brothers of Springfield, Massachusetts. Only one of the Benz finished, a full hour and a half after Frank Duryea completed the fifty-mile course in nine hours. Each car was required to carry a driver and a judge. Along with their $2,000 prize, the Duryeas won invaluable publicity. Their automobile had defeated the best of Europe and the horses as well! The two brothers returned to Massachusetts and set up shop. In 1896 they hand-built and sold thirteen cars, marking the beginning of American automobile production. It is fun to imagine what John's life would have been like if his car had held and he had won the race. He would have received the publicity and the accolades; he would have gone into production instead of the Duryeas; and he would be known today without controversy as the inventor of America's gasoline automobile. The 1891 three-wheeled model we know from one photograph would be in the Smithsonian and I would not be writing this book!

With the success of his race, Editor Kohlstaat achieved more than notoriety for the automobile. He made the disparate inventors aware of each other, congealing a network to foster ideas and production. Kohlstaat also ran a contest for the best name to replace the awkward moniker "horseless carriage". The winner "motorcycle" never caught on. Other offerings were "petrocar", "autocar" and "automotor". Other lost names were "motor carriage" or "motor wagon", "road machine" and "quadricycle". It is generally agreed the French coined the word "automobile" around the turn of the twentieth century and that it comes from the Greek word "auto" meaning "self" and the Latin word "mobils" for "moving". I prefer "ottomobile", referring to Nicholas Otto, the inventor of the four-stroke gasoline engine. The Celtic word "carrus" is the derivation of "cart" and "car".

Several important milestones advancing the automobile happened right after the Chicago race. The American Motor League began as an organization dedicated to the advancement of motor vehicles. Traveling shows, circuses and county fairs began to include motor vehicles as a curiosity. And, thirdly, the giant retailer Montgomery Ward began a publicity campaign using an electric vehicle model to help draw the crowds on a promotional tour of its catalog business to small towns and farmlands. Soon after the *Herald Tribune* race the highly regarded Thomas Edison predicted a powerful impact from the automobile and named gasoline-power as the eventual winner over steam and electric. Two new magazines went to press, one of them edited by Herman

Kohlstaat, *The Motorcycle (Automobile) Maker and Dealer* and one month later, the renowned *Horseless Age.*

To be historically correct, there was an earlier American race. In 1878, the Wisconsin legislature proposed an event meant to encourage the development of self-propelled horseless vehicles. They offered a $10,000 prize to whoever first completed their 200-mile course. There were seven entries, but only two started, both steam-powered vehicles; only one finished. It weighed 9,875 pounds. The competition weighed 14,255 pounds! John's 1891 prototype weighed 560 pounds. News items of the event must have heartened would-be inventors like John, for the legislative body was by their act endorsing the viability of a successful self-propelled vehicle.

With written reports of John's attempts to compete in the 1895 Chicago race it is safe to conclude he had a car. Because the reports refer to a three-wheeled car, it is reasonable to assume John had rebuilt his three-wheeled prototype, which gives more credence to the notion that the Original Car was not completely destroyed by fire. So where is the car John took to Chicago? Gone forever, I fear. John refers to his original car in a 1906 newspaper article (Anderson *Herald*). He said he still had it and would rebuild it for curiosity. If he did, there is no evidence. It is more likely he set the idea aside and went on to other things. I think John was not greatly concerned with the physical remnants his ancestors, historians and museum curators would yearn for. I believe he took the pieces and used them as he needed for new ideas. The next prototype would be four-wheeled and appears in 1898. One thing to conclude for sure is that John actively continued his interest in building a marketable horseless carriage throughout these Buckeye engine years.

It took a long time in the beginning of the automotive age for the public and the automakers to decide on our present-day four-wheeled, engine-in-the-front, gasoline-powered design. The very first auto entrepreneurs faced undefined possibilities. The market culture was an open frontier. Through newspapers and journals the population witnessed the competition among steam, gasoline and electric propulsion that continued well into the twentieth century. Overlaying this early competition was nostalgia for the horse. By the end of the nineteenth century, while many folks said farmers and rural dwellers would never give up their workhorses, American preference was definitely moving away from depending on this old four-legged friend. The car market of the early twentieth century consisted of hundreds of small shops and factories, producing and selling perhaps three machines, perhaps 300, and eventually a few, 3,000. Each year more automobiles were sold and little by little our roads improved. It was not until the Eisenhower Administration did Americans organize a comprehensive highway system. At the same time that John was working on his project of getting a Lambert-designed car to market, other auto designers were placing their prototypes up for sale and making profits on their production. Among the early successful builders of gasoline-powered automobiles were the Duryeas, Alexander Winton and Ransom Olds. Quickly came salable models from Packard, Elgin, Peerless and many others. In 1899, Winton was the largest maker of gasoline-powered cars with one hundred cars. They were open-ride two-passenger touring cars with a two-speed transmission that sold for $1,000. The largest producer of electrics outsold him, 200 to one.

Ransom Olds, who on occasion dined with the Lamberts in Anderson, began designing his curved dash runabout in 1899 and went into production in 1901. He used a single cylinder Sintz engine. His cars became American icons, embedded as a craze in our culture with the 1905 ditty "In My Merry Oldsmobile." In the four year period 1901-1905 Ran sold an astonishing 12,000 of these basic cars at $650 each, the best selling car before Ford's Model T. His curved-dash Oldsmobile buggy was the first truly popular car.

1899 saw thirty American outfits produce 2500 cars for the American market, for a total of 8,000 cars on mostly unpaved roads. Of those 8,000+ vehicles, more than half were electric. In 1900, of the slightly less than 14,000 cars owned by Americans,

40% were steam-powered, 38% were electric and only 22% were gasoline powered. It took some time for gasoline to be established as the fuel of choice of American consumers and manufacturers. I believe it won out because it was plentiful and cheap. The advantages for the individual driver were that the gasoline motor endured longer than the electric and was safer than the steam. Today with gasoline no longer plentiful or cheap, I am sure John would tell us present-day Americans to find another way. Just as the farm boy inventors of the Industrial Age did, we should innovate our way to a new fuel age. We need to develop other fuels and technologies to solve our transportation needs. John was not wedded to gasoline; he chose it for practical reasons. I believe he would counsel us to abandon it today for practical reasons.

As the last decade of the nineteenth century rolled by (or clopped by hoof), the Lambert Gas and Gasoline Company in Anderson and the Union Manufacturing Company in Union City were both successful companies. As the daily worker on the factory floor produced various models of gasoline engines, the carriage parts business flourished under the same Lambert management. Four Lambert brothers were involved and possibly all six, with George keeping up with his sons. John was involved in both locations, carriage-making and engine design, and both enterprises contributed to his own personal project of developing a salable horseless carriage.

In 1898, John built a four-wheeled, two-cylinder prototype that he called the Union. It was intended as a gift for his daughter Mae. As was the custom back then, the brothers/uncles probably used her vehicle to troll for orders with plans to set up production if there were sufficient interest and they could collect enough orders to make a profit. Mae's car was exhibited in 1902 at a Chicago show and received a complimentary write-up in *Carriage Trade* magazine. Reports vary as to when the Lamberts sold their first car. Trade shows of the era, like racing, were marketplace spotlights for automobiles. This was only the beginning of car shows, so it was a process for the promoters to get organized. The earliest show I read about was the National Automobile Show in Madison Square Garden in 1900 where 34 brands of automobiles were displayed. A display in the same venue six years later in 1906 had 220 exhibits. Like today these shows were a way to display ideas, get feedback from others in the business and gauge public reaction. It was definitely possible to collect enough orders at a show to return home, build a facility and start production. No doubt the brothers used smaller stunts to promote the Union as well, like racing or towing loads. I tend to believe that the Chicago trade show was the kick off for Lambert car production. I found no records of Lambert promotional activity until it, and after it, sales for the Union took off.

John's first successful commercial models rolled out of the Union City plant in 1902. This new enterprise in the budding automobile industry was named the Union Automobile Company; John was President. The Lamberts used their own engines manufactured in Indiana by the Lambert Gas and Gasoline Engine Company shipped by rail through Muncie and Winchester to the Ohio factory. There, the engines were fitted to the Union body. The first models had 2-cylinder, 4 cycle, 22 horsepower gasoline-powered engines placed in the back of the vehicles. In later models, the engine was located in the middle of the automobile. A unique feature of the Union was how the front board folded down to accommodate two additional passengers. These little machines were four-seaters. Could this be the source of Al's idea for a pullout sofa bed that he patented in 1909 called the "couch-bed"? Also unique to the Union was a mechanism that enabled the driver to start the engine while sitting behind the wheel, long before Charles Kettering famously put his electric starter in the 1923 Cadillac. The most unique feature, and controversial too, was the gearless transmission. John used his perpendicular disks from the start. The Unions were strong, small vehicles.

Mae was sixteen when she received her car and learned to drive it herself. It went up to 30 mph. She is most likely America's first female gas car owner. John also built a prototype for Ray a few years later, a red turtleback Ray took to college making him the first car owner on the DePauw campus. I can only image the swagger of the nineteen-year old, all 5'5" of him, as he rode this red car around campus attracting admiration from women and men alike.

By 1902 the Lamberts were ready for success with their automobile. They had their design, factory space, their organization and orders on file. Production began. I can't imagine the pride and excitement John felt, along with his family, about getting a car to market. Their numbers soon rose to ten cars per month. From this first automobile production, the Lamberts sold high-end cars made to appeal to people of means. While other makes went for as low as $350, the Unions sold for up to $3,000. There were eight models and in the next two years John and his family sold fifteen hundred Unions, a large number for standards then. One source reported that the 1903 Union could be ordered from outlets from across the nation and carried another unique feature which has been recently revived: they were guaranteed for one year.

A line by America's favorite poet Henry Wadsworth Longfellow gave the Lamberts their motto: "In Union There is Strength." I am proud of their choice. The line appears in an early verse of *Hiawatha* at a point in the story when the various Indian leaders have gathered to hear the voice of their God, who urges them to overcome their fighting amongst themselves because they will soon be confronted by a powerful outside force. "All your strength is in your union." It is a line that jumped out at me as an important admonition for all of us today even before I learned my ancestors had adopted it to their automobiles.

Henry Ford, three years John's junior, had tried to produce a marketable horseless carriage in 1896 and failed. The anecdote is famous: he built it inside a shed and had to take an axe to the shed wall to get it onto the street. Once outside, it did run. But it didn't sell. He then turned to automobile racing to get attention for his ideas. He built racers and competed, sometimes driving himself, whenever he could against men who were already successful automobile manufacturers. In 1904 Ford drove his Model B across a frozen lake and won headlines with a new speed record, 91.37 miles per hour. His big success and the start of his fame in automobile production however did not begin until 1913. This is the year he began mass production of the already popular Model T.

In 1879 a Rochester, New York lawyer designed but did not build a gasoline-powered vehicle. He obtained a patent on his design in 1895 that gave him exclusive rights to manufacture an automobile powered by an internal combustion engine. Known as the Sheldon patent, after George B. Sheldon, each automobile sold in America until 1909 was behooved to pay a royalty to Mr. Sheldon. The largest manufacturers organized into the Association of Licensed Automobile Manufacturers in 1903 to work with Sheldon to restrict newcomers. Henry Ford took them all on and finally won his case in 1911. By breaking the hold on the established car makers, whether he intended to or not, 48-year-old Henry Ford struck a blow for democracy. Being released of paying Sheldon royalties stimulated early car manufacture. Ford went on to manufacture cars by the thousands. His Model T was cheap, easy to drive and available. It gave the worker the same opportunity to travel as the well-(w)heeled boss.

Other events mark the ascension of the automobile: The first US President to ride in a car was William McKinley in a Stanley Steamer, 1899. In 1907, five years before being President, Woodrow Wilson warned that automobiles would "spread socialist feelings in this country." He ate those words and bought a Model T in 1919. The first car to be kept at the White House belonged to President H. Taft.

Dr. Horatio Jackson's 63-day ride across the continental United States was in 1903. The PBS special on his road trip "Horatio's Ride" showed the dramatically difficult conditions he met including rivers, mountains, no roads, angry Indians, hapless locals, rain, snow and other inclement weather, a broken axle and many ruined tires. Although he and his companions, Sewall

Crocker and a dog, endured hardship, the trip became a media spectacle prompting thousands to line the street as he passed through populated areas. Two car manufacturers put vehicles on the road with Jackson, making it a race, but Jackson beat them to the finish. In 1901 Ran Olds sponsored a man to drive his Curved Dash auto from Detroit to New York to establish its mechanical excellence. The driver took the tow road by the New York Erie Canal, a sight I would have liked to see. The first Federal Aid Road Act was not until 1916 and was of course limited against the reality of the vast muddy sea of American roads. Partial help came again not until the Federal Highway Act of 1922. It was not until 1956 that a comprehensive interstate highway program got underway. Good roads or not, Americans were waking up to the driving experience, climbing on board the new individual vehicles and getting behind gasoline-powered transportation.

Chapter 8

The Car Manufacturing Years

The Lambert Car Years (1902-1917) must have been happy years for John Lambert. He found a market for a gasoline-powered automobile of his design and manufacture. The fifteen-year period of Lambert car production pushed John to the pinnacle of the industry. He saw his ideas come to fruition and his automobiles were used by Americans across the land. He sold his first automobiles out of Union City, Ohio in 1902 and in 1903 they were available to order at outlets from California to New York. In 1904 he changed the name of his product and established the Lambert Automobile Company in Anderson, Indiana as that region became America's first automotive hub. In 1902 John's dream of producing individual motorized vehicles dated back over thirteen years. Did he know the automobile would eventually replace the horse? Did he ever imagine the ribbons of roads that would crisscross this land? Sales of his designs made him a rich man. John Lambert did become famous as a car maker, but not as the Inventor of the Original Car. His cars were heralded for their luxury and strength, and his moniker was Father of the Gradual Transmission.

In the same way transmission types are debated today – standard or automatic, the first generation of car owners debated the relative merits of their available designs. Most common was what later was called the standard transmission with its separate clashing gears and disjointed rhythm. Fraught with pauses, the standard transmission used by most car manufacturers back then had more jerk than today. Users of the gear transmission needed to defend their decision not to change to a re-vamped system and so cast doubts about John's radical new technology. In contrast to their methods was John's friction drive with its smooth, even acceleration. It was advertised as having "no gears to grind or strip...no clutch to slip." Controversial because it was gearless, it nonetheless had a large following of satisfied supporters. John's method of acceleration was achieved by running a spinning disk perpendicularly across the face of the fly wheel disk, the face of which was covered with a patented composition plate that took John years to perfect. The friction wheel was set directly on this plate, the shaft which carries it being placed parallel to the center, so the movement was back and forth along the flywheel. The final drive was by chain which connected the rear axle and the friction wheel. The friction wheel was moved by a controller lever at the hand of the driver. The action upon contact between the two disks was unhesitant acceleration that increased by an unbroken progression; slowing down was likewise fluid. Speed could be maintained at any point along the contact line between the two large disks. To one side of center was the forward motion; by crossing the center the car entered reverse. Thus John's system was referred to as "The Car With a Thousand Speeds". The burgeoning automotive media covered the debate.

I do not know what sparked John's imagination and got him to visualize one disk perpendicular to the other. Or to spin them up against each other. My guess is he observed the action in an accidental context and then drew out the acceleration principal. Perhaps this happened at the sawmill on his lumberyard north of Ohio City. In the one photograph I have seen of that site there is a large spinning saw. Its action may have started him on a line of thinking as pieces of wood shot away from the saw's teeth. In their promotional literature the Lamberts liken the principal of the friction drive transmission to the steel-on-steel friction of railroad cars on their track. Americans at the time were familiar with the recent national debate over wooden rails vs. new steel rails. Progressives had wanted the old wooden rails replaced with steel tracks or at least to cap the wood with steel strips. Opponents argued the steel wheels of the train could not grip the steel rail and argued that gear teeth would be necessary on the locomotive driving wheels that would mesh with teeth on the rails. Wiser engineers proved them wrong and Americans learned a lesson about friction drive. Steel replaced the wooden rails. Much of the public now knew from the railroad debate to recognize the line of contact between steel and steel. Lambert literature asked, "Why not deliver your product...in the same way?" Whatever was the source of John's visualizations, the idea of the gearless transmission was simple and unique and it worked. John was successful in overcoming people's prejudices to the extent of other manufacturers adopting the friction drive. For each of those vehicles sold, Lambert got a kickback.

As John concentrated on his friction drive system he aimed for simplicity and quality. For example, the cast-iron fly wheel was bulky and heavy, so John, the story goes, asked the superintendent of the Lambert foundry to cast a wheel of aluminum to make it as light as possible. The aluminum worked exceptionally well. John studied different metal transmitting qualities to develop the fiber plate for the flywheel that would produce maximum power on all speeds. His first idea was to use leather but the heat of the friction charred it. A wood fiber disc lasted 300 miles which was not good enough. By 1900 John had developed a "straw board" fiber that ran great for 2,000 miles and cost $2.80 to replace. By 1907 John had a plate that lasted 3,000 miles.

Into the very first Lambert models produced for market, John installed his perpendicular disks and prominently advertised his friction system of transmission. Unlike prevailing conventional wisdom which focused on costs, John's marketing philosophy emphasized the car's simplicity of design as more important than a lower selling price. He took the long view that people who witnessed his well-performing cars would become customers, a philosophy that bore fruit. Every year John sold more of his cars and he earned his reputation for simplified mechanics without sacrificing strength or efficiency. His designs strove to maintain low upkeep and maintenance costs for the future owner. John designed his car with the owner/mechanic in mind because these pioneer car owners were on their own for repairs. Local repair shops were a thing for the future. All parts were accessible on John's cars so that it was not necessary to crawl under the car to make adjustments. John judged the conventional gear transmission of most other brands to be a complicated system with its high number of parts and therefore a source of mechanical trouble and confusing to repair. So he built a better one. John knew the friction drive was simpler than the geared transmission and would perform well with minimum attention. Top materials for his automobiles were always used: better iron, better steel, better tires, better everything.

The Lambert Buckeye engine, already a well-known brand of gasoline engine, powered the early Union cars. The Buckeye Manufacturing Company and the Lambert Gas and Gasoline Engine Company in Anderson made the engines that were shipped by railroad to the Union Automobile Company in Union City, Ohio where the final product was assembled. Shipments of five or six engines went out regularly. They used a two-cylinder, four-cycle balanced type engine with the crankshaft in its middle and a piston at either end. By this arrangement, one piston balanced the other which helped create a ride free of vibration. Each vehicle was fitted with a jump spark ignitor, although a touch-spark system could be ordered in its stead. Either way the motor was started with the help of a dry battery from the driver's seat; the electricity and action was actuated by the foot of the operator. There was no cranking necessary for the early Union cars. The start was smooth, unlike the "jerk start" of other makers.

John took pride in appearances as well as in his well-devised mechanics. Like John's 1891 prototype, the Union was a trim and clever car with black leather upholstery. The fuel tank was completely hidden behind the seat, leaving a clean line for the back of the automobile. The sales brochure describes the fuel tank as holding enough "for a run of from 125 to 150 miles." These cars were built to go the distance. The cooling system was efficient, using only a small amount of water running through a double coil radiator. Following themes he founded in the beginning of his career this model was light and stylish, with a smooth, steady ride and at the same time was roomy, powerful and as fast as 60 mph. The high backseat provided comfort to the driver and the rider and a look of stability to the observer. With the engine in the rear or under the seat, the front of the vehicle was available for optional accommodations for two more passengers by folding down the floorboard over the front axle to show two more cushions. To me, these two positions look hazardous so close to the uneven road, from bouncing bums, on-coming bugs and upturned pebbles. It looks about as safe as riding on a bicycle handlebars. To those of the day, it must have been a good way to add room for two more riders.

Overall the car sounds like a practical first car for America. Hard working and reliable with clever engineering and design that was easy to drive and simple to care for, John's car was its own best advertisement to convince the public to "motor-vate". The strength of John's belief in his product, along with innovators like him, led the way into the Automobile Age as these early engineers convinced Americans to give up their horses and try a machine instead. And yet, my Dad recalled, "Grandfather didn't think he set the world on fire by putting wheels under a gasoline engine."

In 1903, the year after John established his presence in the market, there were less than 33,000 automobiles registered to drivers in the entire country. (Compare to 230 million registered American drivers in 2005.) Roads were still very primitive. The industry was just coming into existence. It had been less than ten years since the Duryea's sold their first handmade horseless carriage. David Buick began selling his cars in 1901 as did Ran Olds. Other known names were yet to be. GM was not founded until 1908. Ford's first sales were in 1903, but the assembly line and his explosive success would not happen until 1914. The earliest car show I read about had been in 1900. The 1902 car show in Chicago featured many new models, including the famous Rambler Runabout. John Lambert and his family business presented their Union model at this show. A photograph taken there that remains in the Lee collection shows the Union display next to Moon, also a new entry to the market that was destined to make a showing. Another old name familiar to some but now long gone, the Premier debuted with the Union. Many of the established models on the market at this time were electric like Stanley and Locomobile. In 1899 Pope was the biggest manufacturer with 2,093 cars, half of the cars made that year. The top of the Union line went for a whopping $3,000. That sum in 1902 was equivalent to $75,000 today. On at least one agents' wall was the sign, "You Auto Take One Home With You."

The car John took to display in Chicago was the handsome model he had made for his daughter, a two-seater painted white. Mechanically, it performed wonderfully for all to see. *Motor World* magazine reviewed the Chicago Show in February 17, 1903 saving highest praise for the Union "because of the truly marvelous demonstration it made with a *Motor World* man as passenger." The ride the reporter went on was described,

> With this engine and this transmission a *Motor World* man was taken first up the Water Street hill, from the Erie depot, next down the hill by the viaduct to where the Detroit and Buffalo boat landings are. Two thirds down this latter hill the engine was reversed and the car easily backed the entire way up the hill, never faltering for an instant or making any fuss whatever.

> To anyone who knows this grade the performance can be appreciated. Sufficient to say it is one of the steepest to be found anywhere.

After this the Lake Shore depot hills were easy, though they both are climbs of the severest kind. No attempt whatever was made to "rush" them, the car simply keeping on its way up the same even rate of speed of which it had been traveling.

There was absolutely no vibration, no pounding, no strain. The facts speak for themselves, and are given simply because they are facts and of the kind that are thought worthy of recording.

I bet the driver was John. Two-thirds down the hill he moved it into reverse, confident the car would respond smoothly and go backwards up the hill, which it did. Do not try this today.

Sweet-faced and spunky, John's daughter Mae told the story in her later years of driving her unusual means of transport in the olden days around the streets of Anderson where she grew up. The teenage boys, she said, flocked to the sight and she offered them driving lessons. She must have had a lot of fun showing off her driving dexterity and automobile knowledge to the clamoring fellas. There was only one other female driver in town, Mae reported, and she on a Stanley Steamer. The fact that John did this for his daughter is a family legend. "He made his daughter a car!" Both Lee and Lambert sides of the family that I grew up knowing repeated this: "He made his daughter a car!" And the fact that this car was the prototype for John's automotive success propelled the legend. With her shiny brown hair, Mae must have made a marvelous advertizement behind the wheel of her customized white roadster with enough room for a rider on the red leather beside her and with a little rumble seat behind her. It had black striping and beautiful thirty-inch wooden artillery wheels, two large gas lamps and two oil lamps. All lamps were brass and beveled clear glass.

The Union's debut was a smashing success. After the Chicago trade show production began at ten cars a month. This was a strong start. Within a year Unions were being ordered for one hundred dollars down with payment due upon delivery. Unlike their competition, the Lambert Union had a one-year guarantee.

John used today's popular ploy in 1902. I wonder who thought up the guarantee; it was likely John's brother Al. No record remains.

Ray told the story of a brouhaha over production numbers. In 1903 Lambert advertised in *Horseless Carriage* that they would build 950 cars in the coming year. This caused a furor! Ray named Alexander Winton as "scared". He declared the total number of cars sold in the entire country could certainly not reach that number! Lambert would glut the market. There were calls for a voluntary cap on production at which the Lamberts laughed. Winton and the others could not imagine the popularity of the Curved Dash which jumped from selling 425 cars in 1901 to 4,000 cars in 1903. In spite of the industry's skepticism, Lambert sold every one of their projected output. The market base was exploding. Lambert was an early leader in the numbers game. It was such a different world back then. Today's output numbers are staggering in comparison. The way deals were made also seem casual compared to today. Ray told a story of being in a barber shop in New York with Will Durant, the founder of GM who was getting a shave. Ray watched as a fellow approached Durant with a design for a car and before the barber was done, Durant had bought the design for $150,000.

As the family had done a decade earlier with the initial success of their stationery-model gasoline engine, the Lamberts acted quickly to make the most of their high sales demand by planning an immediate expansion. To meet their market, they re-organized their two locations. In 1903 they made the decision to expand and consolidate by moving all automotive operations to Anderson, Indiana. They would still produce buggy and carriage parts in Union City. They paid $150,000 for five acres of land along Columbus Avenue in Anderson and enlarged their production space to 450,000 square feet. With all the up-to-date equipment and machinery The Anderson *Herald* described the new factory as "probably superior to anything of the kind in the State." They hired 350-400 workers. In order to maximize the use of natural light, the space was built out, not up, so their building took the shape of a large horseshoe.

On May 2, 1905 The *Herald* reported that the first automobile was under construction at the new Lambert factory. The same article reported the Union City foreman, George Spencer, was now moved to Anderson and in charge in the new landmark building. Expansion continued through 1905 as the Lambert factory was fitted with new machinery for making engines for "farm and travel." While still producing Unions, John set up the Lambert Automobile Manufacturing Company and the name switch was made in 1905. The new models called Lambert were identical to the Union but soon the line expanded with larger four-cylinder models. Although there would be no more, I estimate John sold 1,500 Unions before the name was changed. I know of none that exist today although photos are plentiful. He was now established in the marketplace as an automaker. The new Lambert model was an immediate hit and moved John up the ladder of success.

It would have been fun to see the Unions and then the Lamberts leaving the Anderson factory by the back door right out onto the railroad loading dock, to watch them go up onto flatbed railroad cars before taking off for maybe Milwaukee or Kansas City. I read a *Herald* article of 1905 that described a shipment of two carloads: "the machines were the largest ever made in Anderson and two of the big autos made a carload." I was reading media coverage for the shipment of four cars! This was truly a "Start" for the huge worldwide industry we know today. To the Lamberts of Indiana, two carloads of two cars each was a big order. St. Louis became a big market and the family businessmen floated stories about opening a factory there. I have seen an old Lambert letterhead that shows Lambert facilities with a St. Louis address but the building in the picture used is mysteriously the same as the Anderson plant. Ah, well, the Lamberts were ambitious and wishing is almost getting there. I guess locally manufactured goods sold better. No, there were no manufacturing facilities in St. Louis, but sales were significant, like in other areas.

I imagine myself at the factory in Anderson standing to the side watching the trailer being loaded with those elegant cars off to the right of me while behind me on Columbus Street are the occasional, familiar carts and wagons, horses and carriages and lots of folks on foot or with bikes. The March 22, 1914 issue of the Indianapolis *Star* describes the Lambert factory: "Raw materials enter at one end of the factory, pass through various construction departments and emerge at the opposite end in the shape of completed cars ready for shipment." Having gone through the various construction departments in the interior of the plant, the completed cars emerge at the back door. Shipments of Lambert cars were going out routinely. I know this is the picture of John's success: models of his design, manufactured under his processes, going out the door to new owners across the county.

On July 6 of 1905, the Anderson *Morning Herald* carried an article reporting accolades for John's performance with a Lambert car in a five-day endurance race from Chicago to St. Paul. Of fifty-three entrants, John came home with the second place trophy along with tributes to his car's performance. The article said, "The winner was a White Steamer, so the Lambert was the first gasoline-powered automobile to finish. The success of the 16 h.p. Lambert against some 40 h.p. automobiles was attributed to the Lambert Friction Drive." I have long seen a photograph showing a delighted John under a poncho behind the driver's seat of a big, beautiful machine covered in mud. I now believe this photo was taken after this race. Must have been! I can tell by his smile! Later that month the newspaper reported the Lambert Company's shipment of large, expensive Lambert cars and "autotrucks" to Baltimore, Maryland. The company, it reported, was producing ten machines every twenty-four hours. I found an old car ad on the Internet for a "National 40", a Lambert touring car that sold for $2,500. The ad claimed this model had just competed in a "meet" and drew "two firsts, four seconds, two thirds." The National had a 4 cylinder motor and a 124" wheelbase. The Lambert National was a sturdy machine, and was called "The fastest and most powerful stock car in the world." Sales skyrocketed for Lambert high-grade cars. Between 1900 and 1910 car racing mesmerized the nation and propelled all car sales. If Germany gave birth to the automobile and France rocked the cradle, here in America was its thrill-crazed adolescence. Breaking speed records became a mania and the daredevil drivers of these machines were heroes. More than the horse, automobiles were pitted against railroad locomotives and headlines told of the new, individual vehicles traveling at "railway speed." Americans wanted speed and power; John Lambert of Anderson, Indiana delivered both.

To prove to the public that these new machines were worth the bother of owning, John orchestrated shows of strength for the work his vehicles could do. He organized educational campaigns to demonstrate the car's ability to live up to its motto: "In Union There is Strength." His background as a farm worker lent appreciation for a vehicle's workability. In addition, the Lamberts knew continued sales depended on proving that the demand for the auto was not just a craze. He wanted his public to know his cars could do the job. For the demonstrations, John liked to do the driving himself. He personally drove one of his Lambert models up the steps of the courthouse in Chicago. I saw a picture of their Chicago Rep behind the wheel of a Lambert 5-seater who was climbing the steps of the local McKinley High School, a demonstration he often made. This escapade was widely duplicated and often successful in drawing publicity.

I have read in more than one place about the driving ability of my great-grandfather. In a 1904 driving demonstration for a writer of *Cycle and Automobile Trade Journal* John inspired the man to write that behind the wheel my great-grandfather was "demonic". I imagine at the time he was rather determined to make the most of the opportunity to show off while at the same time confident he could do that. The writer, Horace L. Arnold (aka Hugh Dolnar), sized up the performance in glowing terms. John had nerves of steel and could offer an impressive ride to the right passenger. In one performance for a group of farmers John hitched a car to a plow. Completing against a two-horse team John put the friction transmission to work and kept up with the equine pair. He participated in dead weight contests. The competing autos would hitch themselves each to a heavy stationery object and attempt to pull it a distance. With its spinning wheels' high percentage of power efficiency, John's friction drive did exceptionally well against the standard transmission. The weights would strip the standard gears of the other cars. Likewise other car makers staged stunts to drum up publicity and sales, but John had a special ferociousness. He was particularly eager to show the others that his transmission design was not just viable but advantageous to the standard transmission. 1901 was the year Ran Olds had his Curved Dash auto driven from Detroit to New York along the picturesque tow road by the New York Canal, a publicity stunt to establish its mechanical excellence in the public's mind. In relation to John, Scott Bailey said "automotive journals and newspapers around 1910 recorded hundreds of public tests demonstrating the ability of the gearless friction car to be driven up 50% ramp inclines and the steps of courthouses."

Not everyone was enthusiastic about driving around in the new cars. John's tiny wife approached the trembling, rattling, lurching machines with trepidation and stepped up to the sideboard as though the act were an acrobatic feat. Cranking an engine was out of the question for her; perhaps this is why John built cars whose engines could be started at the driver's seat. Minnie was reluctant but she did get in the vehicles and even drove John's cars by herself. I have no reports of her skills behind the wheel but I heard stories about her attitude. Always strongly opinionated, she had her own perceptions of her husband's automobiles and she did not trust a self-propelled vehicle to climb a hill. She had John stop at the bottom so she could get out with the children and the three of them walked up to where John waited with the vehicle at the top. She had a rule, "Don't take me out of town," based on the fear that the car would break down and/or that in the expansive landscape John would drive fast. As cars became more widely used in general, we know she relented and became more accepting of her husband's new fangled horseless carriages.

John designed and his workers built on the property across from the factory a unique colossal wooden structure for showing off the strength of a Lambert built vehicle. It was tagged "the greatest structure of the sort ever erected." Basically an elevated roadway, its ramp angled up at 45 degrees to a level 15 feet in the air and extended 30 feet long, at which place there began a set of iron steps for regaining ground level. It was high and narrow; it looked like the first big hill of a giant roller coaster made of a giant erector set. The promotional photograph I looked at includes four men standing on the structure near and at the top. This clearly illustrated the height and scale of the incline. And a frightfully high structure it was, representing a hair-raising ride! I swoon to imagine the sight of the handsome, hefty-built car maker, now in his mid-forties, driving his two-ton machine with the same casual confidence he had as a thirty-year-old in his three-wheeled 530 pound buggy, moving the levers at his hands and feet, allowing the spinning disks to engage the 4-cylinder engine to take the incline as it pulled the load up the narrow path of the wooden planks. In another picture of the structure, a Lambert truck is shown climbing up one side of the steep incline, silhouetted against a clear sky, with my great-grandfather behind the wheel. His feat was to fix in the minds of a horse-centered populace that a Lambert vehicle can get you there quicker and easier, while pulling a heavy load and going uphill! I read every Lambert auto that was produced at the factory was tested "on the ramp". From a sales brochure comes this testimonial from an outfit in Hamilton, Ohio, American Scale and Tank Company:

Dear Sir: No doubt you would be interested in knowing something regarding our experience with the large Lambert "friction-drive" truck which we have had in use of several months.

We operate a very large plant, the production of which must be great enough to fill the orders of a sales organization numbering 240 men. This will give you some idea as to the amount of trucking we have to do, more especially when you realize that our regular plant is located about a mile from the railroad, in addition to which we operate an iron and brass foundry located about one-half mile from the railroad, the production of which this truck must also handle.

Our system of foundries and manufacturing plants is such that the truck has received especially hard usage, due to the fact that it not only handles the manufactured products, but also the result of the foundry production which, of course means heavy, rough work.

We are glad to state that this Lambert "friction-drive" truck has not only performed this service in the most excellent and satisfactory manner, but has far exceeded our every expectation. The cost of maintenance is so much less than our previous cost of handling this business through the medium of the ancient "horse-power" route that we hesitate to give you any figures, for the reason that one not well advised or not on the ground and in a position to have the actual personal experience would hardly believe such figures to be correct.

We believe the best evidence of our faith, founded on our experience in the Lambert "friction-drive" truck, is best proven in the fact that we shortly expect to place an order for another.

Perhaps this proven efficiency could be of help today.
From Bargersville, Indiana, the Rush Brothers wrote:

In reply to yours of the 29th, in which you ask how we like our truck, will say that it is giving us good service. We have a Lambert passenger car that we have operated since last May, and the engine is now working better than it did when we first ran the car out of the shop. We have run the car something over five thousand miles and our bill for gas, oil and batteries has been $42.00, which is less than one cent per mile...

As to our new truck we have discarded all of our horses and depend on the truck altogether, which we can do in less than half the time we did the same business with the team of horses. We certainly think the Lambert machine is a grand success, and we are proud to recommend it to anyone needing a truck. There is one thing about the Lambert truck that can be relied on and that is the power of the engine. We have taken our truck this winter when the streets and roads were in the worst condition and hauled our coal for both our stores and went over the roads where the farm wagon could not go.

We, as business men, have no desire to misrepresent this matter at all, and all we ask of anyone is to call at our place and see the machines work. With best wishes for your success with the Lambert.

"Our bill for gas, oil and batteries . . was less than one cent per mile." Wow! John knew from his farming background now coupled with his manufacturing expertise the nature of work Americans faced across the country and so he sold a sturdy, efficient vehicle ready for the tasks.

By 1906 the Lamberts were producing cars, fire engines, trucks and tractors. Being at the factory sounds like a gearhead dream. A lot of exciting things were being done on the large cement floor within the brick walls of the plant, motor assembling, body building, painting, chassis assembling, upholstering, engineering. Across the front of the building facing Columbus Avenue were offices and showrooms. Towards the back there were stock rooms for current work and for a large store of parts of all models, to respond quickly to owners. The Lamberts knew the value of a good reputation and wanted to be known as responsible for their workmanship. This speaks to their commitment to service and follow-through to the owners. The plant was a well-defined system in a well-organized space that was thoroughly equipped for the job at hand with the latest improved lathes and drill presses and other tools including a two-story (the height of the ceiling) indoor crane. Windows filled much of the wall space for a well-lit workspace. The employees were a close-working unit.

One of the treasures of my Car Years research was a 1967 Anderson *Herald* article featuring offspring of Lambert factory workers. These men were repeating to the reporter what they had heard from their fathers, stories of working at the Lambert factory in downtown Anderson before the First World War. They told of secret experiments of streetcars, both urban and interurban, building large pleasure automobiles and custom power wagons, now called trucks. A significant part of Lambert's business was to accommodate the individual entrepreneur or municipality by making custom trucks, vans and buses. For example they made bakery trucks, milk wagons and transport vans, one in particular was used to transport a gospel choir. One story is of a Lambert rail car built for a private citizen Mr. E. H. Harriman to operate between his house and the Erie Railroad. Another source listed two Lambert street cars produced and running "in the east" with more street cars in the works. One streetcar pictured in Lambert literature weighed eleven tons empty with a seating capacity of thirty-five passengers. It had a 150 HP engine and a Lambert Patented Friction Transmission. This tag said the cars had been in operation for several years in different parts of the country. I like thinking that certain cities and towns scattered across the country bought Lambert street cars to offer transportation to their public. There were plenty of years in my life when I depended upon municipal buses. The era brought many civic schemes to provide transportation services and the Lamberts joined in conspiracy to develop products for municipalities, business and government, and individuals, including a gasoline motorcar designed to also run on existing railroad tracks.

These former Lambert workers told their sons about building a large prototype called a "railbus" that could travel on rails or the street. To the men of the interview, their fathers had been engaged in many exciting enterprises and to me, too. Even the few words quoted in the article are fascinating for the mental pictures they paint and evoke the buzz of excitement that must have surrounded these old endeavors. They were building machines that were a radical new technology. Reading about the legacy of these men extends a human touch to the experience of being involved in the manufacture of these early automobiles and brings to life the photographs I have seen of these one-of-a-kind vehicles. I imagine the laughter and yelling in the factory joining the routine noises and smells of the work on the floor as these pre-World War One skilled factory workers, many of them Lambert family members and/or long time Lambert employees, with their sweat and muscle and their keen senses, constructed their wares. The men whose sons reminisced were an integral part of America's rapidly developing transportation industry. As well as tales of short-lived ideas, they told of the successful manufacture of fire engines and fire trucks, gas and gasoline engines, steel-hoofed tractors and of course hundreds and hundreds of work trucks and automobiles.

Many photographs mentioned in this book were printed in a series of articles in the Anderson *Herald* in the 1960's by Man About Town author Gene Boch, sports editor, city editor and managing editor for the Anderson paper. His Man About Town columns on John Lambert recount the history of John's achievement of inventing the first gasoline-powered automobile in America and his career as an automotive industrialist. He highlights the unusual prototypes the Lambert factory worked on and gave his readers a good description of an Anderson hero, the Inventor of America's First Car.

George Lambert, John's father, started the Lambert focus on work machines. He established a successful enterprise manufacturing and selling farm tools and wagon parts and his sons continued to develop machinery useful to the farmer and working entrepreneur. From poles and shafts their cornerstone had become the production of gasoline engines which continued parallel to their luxury car business. Even though it took a decade for it to happen, I bet when George saw John's first gasoline engine he could and did visualize his inventive son's eventual success with his horseless carriage. George, John's father, did live to see his son's dream come true; he died in 1906 in his eightieth year. The Urbana farm where John was born was sold in 1913. In a similar way that the rich Ohio soil lay ready for George to farm when he arrived from the mountains of Cambria County, Pennsylvania, the American public, largely isolated and scattered but curious and itchy to roam, lay ready for John to sell them cars. John's mother died early in 1902; she, too, probably heard car production being planned and knew it was in the works. She surely had seen her granddaughter in her unusual machine, the original prototype, and probably rode in it herself. Both of John's parents were around to know of his automotive success. What a life span they witnessed! This is the couple that likely used their own two feet to get from Pennsylvania to Ohio before the Civil War and they lived to see from their own front porch the dawn of the Automobile Age.

Sources of the era reported that John experimented with airplane technology. There is a photograph, published in several places, showing him standing at the Old Fairgrounds in Anderson beside a bi-plane with Mr. Charles Hensley at the controls and both wives standing nearby. In one book John is incorrectly identified as his brother Cal, but I recognize John and Minnie. This is the source that states the plane was in the air for ten seconds, before the Wright Brothers. Mr. Hensley was a test driver for Lambert. Could he have flown that plane? Did John work on that plane? Did it in fact have a Lambert engine? The picture invites speculation. Another source said this plane flew with an aluminum Lambert 4-cycle engine in it. Mr. Hensley's son is quoted in a Man About Town article in the *Anderson Herald*, "I remember my father saying he and others were working on the plane and getting ready to try it out when word was received that the Wright Brothers had been in the air." When asked if his father said the plane flew, the son said, "Yes, it was in the air and flew a few feet." This report was shortly after the Wright Brothers flew for 12 seconds over 120 feet in Kitty Hawk.

Some years later John reportedly also collaborated with a Mr. J. F. Wilkinson of Boston and Beverly, Massachusetts on what now would be called a helicopter. A Beverly newspaper announced that Amelia Earhart had plans to visit Mr. Wilkinson and his aircraft in the New England town in 1937. In an astonishing letter she writes, "there would be no time (to visit) before my next planned hop-off.... When I return I shall try and investigate" his plane. Her motive for interest in his invention was, she wrote, "Safety in flying is paramount and I believe radical design will be necessary to move a step further." In a great irony, she was lost on that next flight. The Lee family chest contains a photograph of Mr. Wilkinson's working model he called a "avolater." It was designed to be "glidable" should the engine fail; the four horizontally mounted propellers were tiltable. I wonder what John's hand was in that. As I continued to fill in my understanding of my great-grandfather, one thing is clear: his innovative genius infused all his endeavors. I am proud of his achievements because I believe it is this sprit of discovery and innovation, this expression of individual talent that is the lifeblood of democracy.

Chapter 9

Father of the Gradual Transmission

In 1907 John W. Lambert was President of one of the most successful automobile companies in the country. The Lambert Automobile Company was a prosperous enterprise that many people relied upon for their livelihood. After fifteen years of living in Anderson, John and his wife were pillars of their small Indiana community ten miles from Indianapolis. They had raised their children here and had a large extended family in the area. They were involved in civic and religious organizations and had many social acquaintances including extensive contacts in the mushrooming automobile industry. John had established his wealth and his name. It was not uncommon for less successful men to approach him for his monetary help and guidance. John was not surprised when a particular man contacted him about obtaining some financial backing. Henry Ford worked out of Detroit, at the time a horse and buggy town. At this point Ford had tried selling his models but had had little success. Now he had a prototype he wanted to build he called his Model T. John was interested in the project but not enough to be lured by the Michigander's offer; the deal involved throwing in with money and talent, necessitating being on sight. The well-established fifty-three-year-old from Anderson was selling cars all over the country at a leading rate from where he was and not inclined to relocate. No, I don't think my great-grandfather could have considered Mr. Ford's proposal for more than an instant. Even if he himself flirted with the idea, he knew full well Mrs. Lambert would not be open to relocating. This part of the story my dad was sure of: Minnie was 100% against going to Detroit. What my dad was not clear on was whether Minnie knew of the possibility prior to the decision being made. He recalls she fed the impression the offer held no sway. This may have been her way to belittle comparisons to Ford's wealth and notoriety. At her stage of life she would more likely have been looking forward to being a senior member of her church and involved with her daughter's wedding in their family home than in setting up a new home in a new state.

However, John respected Henry Ford enough to take his plea seriously and wanted to help the eager entrepreneur from Michigan. John viewed this as an opportunity his son might consider. He contacted nineteen-year-old Ray, my grandfather, to discuss the opportunity. Ray was a college student at the time this was happening and no novice to the rough and tumble game of the primitive automobile business. I am not sure if John called him home from school or if the topic waited until the next visit. No night letter survives but my guess is Ray was called home because Mr. Ford was in the process of arranging a meeting of all potential investors. Ray has quoted his father here as describing Ford as "a fellow who wants to build a car in Detroit." John explained the situation to his son and encouraged him to explore the opportunity. After all, Ray's stage of life might be judged more susceptible to the offer than that of John and Minnie. John offered to front Ray the $1,900.00 Ford was looking for should Ray decide it was a worthwhile venture. But the Lambert "work-for-yourself" gene was about to assert itself. When the nineteen-year-old went to the meeting in Detroit where Henry Ford showed the design for his new model and laid out his plans for production, he learned Ford's idea was to sell cars by keeping the mechanics simple and costs extremely low. In that way many more people could afford to buy.

John might have doubted altogether the idea that a car could be affordable by the mainstream. Producing his cars to the highest standards perhaps served John's vanity somehow, for using cheaper materials and/or compromised mechanics for the sake of a less expensive product was definitely less appealing to him. Early in the last century the concept that the automobile was a rich man's toy was well imbedded in society and John was enjoying that market. Ford's plan, John was to learn, involved using a 2-cylinder engine. At this point John's big sellers were 4-cylinders and he believed 4-cylinder machines "were the coming thing." (Auto Pioneer article.) Contented in his own circumstances, as I imagine him, John had nothing to gain by joining Henry Ford's company. Successful, popular and established in Anderson, he had considerable time to pursue his first passion of spending time in his work shed devising better methods and machines. The bottom line, as Dad imagined it, was John preferred to be his own boss. So he sent his son in his stead.

The potential investors who gathered in the various red-leather high back booths of the Detroit restaurant included the Dodge Brothers and Ransom Olds. When Ray returned to Anderson he told his father how Henry Ford made the rounds to each table. Ray acquired a distinct impression of the would-be car maker. One article called their meeting "sometimes stormy" and reported Ray recalled Ford was "wearing a bright plaid tie and a celluloid collar." Salesmanship as a trait runs in my family like brown hair or crooked toes, a trait Ray had studied and developed, so when Ray commented Ford was "not particularly a good salesman" he meant Ford made a horrible impression of his interpersonal skills. Dad tells the story of Ray's return report to his father that included Ray's assessment that "Ford had no charm." A newspaper article described Ray as dubious about Ford because of the man's "just plain cussedness." The insightful nineteen-year-old said he respected Ford's intelligence and intensity, but believed Ford's personality would be too difficult to work with, Dad said. Ray chose to remain under his father's professional roof rather than venture off with a man he "could not respect." He returned to college. In a 1952 article Ray is quoted as saying, "I decided I wouldn't quit school and go up to Detroit with him. I knew very well that he and I would never get along. We'd be in a fight the first day. It never would have worked out." The son of the day's famous car maker did not want to gamble on another man's dream and so chose to remain under the Lambert roof. As a psychotherapist I think it is fascinating John offered his son this generous option to leave the family business. From what I understand, John's years in Ohio City when he was off on his own away from his family were fondly remembered, so that the message of this offer would have been in good faith and thus gave Ray freedom in remaining. It became his choice to stay and work with his father.

Several sources stated John made a final gesture to Ford. After the final Lambert no, John took the trouble to suggest another name to Ford, a man in Detroit who was connected to a Detroit coal firm. I found the name of the man sited in several sources as Mr. James Couzens, but I believe the correct name was in another source from the Indiana Room of the Anderson Public Library. This source said it was Mr. Alexander Y. Malcomson. Mr. Malcomson had been a coal man. He became an original investor and a board member of the Ford Motor Company. As is well known, Henry Ford went on to outrageous financial success developing the moving assembly line, changing the role of the automobile and turning the industry into cultural bedrock. By 1924 half of the cars in the world were Fords. But in spite of the Ford family's fabulous fame and monetary success, I doubt either Lambert, father or son, ever regretted his decision.

I told my teenage son this story out in our driveway as he washed his 1996 Mustang, a beautiful dark satin green vehicle with 225 horsepower in its 4.6-liter V-8 engine, a beloved car he had bought himself. He stopped wiping the seventeen-inch alloy wheels, the white wooly mitts on both hands dripping suds and water, to look at me. Gesturing slightly to the car, he gasped, "You mean this could have been a Lambert Mustang!?"

It's fun to stick my tongue in my cheek and say yes, even if it is a big stretch.

Early in the car sales game there were no dealerships dotting the country that now makes buying a car so accessible. Most cars were sold by mail order. Once a buyer received his (or her) automobile he was on his own. There was no profession of car mechanics the proliferation of which we rely on today. A car owner needed to be a car mechanic as well, a fact that underlines John's sales philosophy. A copy of a popular book published in 1912 called *Motor Car Anatomy* by Franklin Peirce, manufacturer of the Pierce automobile, has been handed down in my family. There are other copies available on the market now. Before that publication, the Lambert organization provided a pamphlet to each car customer written by John's brother Frank who was President of the Company at the time. It was a book really, called *Auto Catechism* in which the maintenance of driving and caring for the automobile is described in easy-to-understand terms. It is an instruction book, a textbook for new owners for operating and maintaining their new machine. Frank explains thoroughly the value of the friction drive transmission. He talks about the rest of the car in a personable and gracious style. John's dedication to simplicity pays off for the public who owned his models, for the maintenance was "so easy a woman could understand." Ouch. Yes, a Lambert brochure said that.

As I was researching sales and distribution methods I found the name and address of a Boston agent, Mr. W. H. Stimson of 33 Broad Street in Boston, dated 1905. This outfit collected orders and arranged for delivery of Lambert vehicles manufactured in Anderson for folks living in Boston and New England. I would so love to come across one of those old automobiles. I have seen old names and return Massachusetts addresses naming Hull, Haverill (Seavey Brothers Sporting Goods) and Roxbury (J.W. Day and

Sons shoes and boots). The building in downtown Boston just a block from Old City Hall out of which those Lambert cars were sold not only exists today but my sister happened to have worked in that very place for a number of years. When I shared the information I had found about our great-grandfather's ties to her former business address, she was amazed.

On a postcard to his sister, my grandfather wrote over a photograph of a popular Lambert model, "She's a peach, Mae and we're selling 'em to beat the band." The popular model was the "Friction Flyer" referring to a very popular Lambert model named after the friction drive transmission. It was advertized as having "up to the minute construction, from the motor to the smallest bolt in the car. It starts easy, rides easier, and costs less."

Ray literally grew up with and within the automobile industry. He came of age as his father's career blossomed and he rode the wave of prosperity along with the entire family. He rode in America's first car as a toddler. He was three when the family lived in Ohio City, Ohio and his father built his three-wheeled wonder. He was fourteen when the first Unions rolled off the block. I imagine John had Ray involved with the company as it developed, as his father had done with him. Ray had a front-row seat for history in the making. My grandfather started college at Ohio University before he transferred to DePauw in Indiana. Mae attended college, too. Young Ray had a stunning red Lambert turtleback car to drive on campus where he was a member of the Phi Kappa Psi fraternity. In a book of Anderson history my grandfather is described as "an avowed enemy of the speed limit." John apparently enjoyed indulging his loved-ones. Aunt Jean Lee told of seeing a diamond bracelet John had brought back to his daughter from a trip to New York City. Aunt Jean guessed Mae was about twelve when she received this generous gift, while her father was manufacturing gasoline engines. It might have been the 1899 trip for which I saw his business expense log that included no mention of jewelry.

Of the very early days, Ray recalled numerous gatherings of
auto makers at the Pontchartain Hotel in Detroit and the breath-
less atmosphere of the early auto shows. In a newspaper interview
my grandfather said, "It was possible to build only one car, ship
it to New York, take customers' orders, and return to Detroit
with enough money to build a plant to turn out the cars." Or,
as his own father did, return to Anderson from Chicago with
enough orders to go into production. In 1912 the Buckeye Manufacturing Company had four owners, three Lambert brothers and
twenty-four year old Ray. Frank was President, John was Treasurer, Al was Secretary and Ray was Vice-President and Director
of Sales. Harry and possibly another brother Cal had developed
auto-related businesses. They had "auto hotels" in Anderson, one
of the many types of axillary businesses that sprang up in con-
junction with automobile sales. Auto hotels offered auto repair
and storage. With no car garages at home, people kept their cars
at an auto hotel to take in and out and stored them there for long
periods over the cold and icy months of the winter. In 1912, there
were different agents representing Lambert in all sections of the
country. My guess is Ray traveled to cities and towns to foster
these contacts and set up additional agents who would find buy-
ers. My father told me about a Lambert car being displayed in the
lobby of a big hotel; probably Ray did this in more than one city.
Agents like Mr. Stimson in Boston established themselves in various cities and brokered orders for more than one manufacturing
outfit and/or bought franchises to be the auto maker's exclusive
rep in the area. In time agents left the hotel lobbies and found
means and space to display cars in specially built showrooms to
lure the public and spread the trend to gasoline-powered vehicles.
The dealership system we have now for selling new cars, from factory to consumer, took time to develop. I'm sure Ray was on hand
at County and State Fairs and other gatherings of rural folks with
Lambert cars, trucks and tractors. In the 1960's I saw my dad put
his own 1910 four-door Lambert tonneau touring car at the Day-

ton Airport in a big raised display to advertise his lawn equipment products.

Lambert cars were fairly expensive but gave good value for the dollar. Handmade and stylish, they were offered with a number of top notch options. The 1910 Lambert touring car had two lighting systems, both kerosene and acetylene gas lamps. The model had doors only for the rear seat. When cars of the era also included doors for the front seat, for example the 1911 Lamberts, the model was said the have "fore doors" and thus was born some confusion over door numbers. The car had "snappy design, sturdy construction and a high-grade finish." Unlike my old mental pictures of the era, cars were colorful! Like most competitors, Lambert autos could be ordered with paint and interior color of the buyer's choosing from a variety of colors. The standard color scheme for 1912 models was a blue black. A deep red body striped with black was popular. I repeated to my dad that I had read about a Lambert with an orange body and black fenders, set off with black striping. A Princeton alum, Dad growled back at me like a tiger. Many Lambert cars were dark green, called "Lambert green". This is a far cry from the practical 1912 Ford which was available in "any color you want as long as it was black." Lambert boasted 26 layers of paint.

Each year manufacturers competed by adding amenities to their models and by changing the design. In 1905 the Lamberts had a horn operated by a foot bellow. The steering mechanism of every brand quickly morphed from a tiller stick to a wheel and by 1914 left-side drive was pretty much standard. Why the left side and not the right, like in Europe? Well, maybe that is in fact why. Another explanation I read was that on the left side the driver had a better view of what is ahead. Most all of John's cars, including my Dad's two models, had right-side drive. There were many incremental changes as the car developed into a version more familiar to today's owners. Doors for the front seat, those "fore doors", were introduced in Lambert's 1911 model and became standard thereafter. The enclosed riding cab did not become standard industry-wide until some time after its introduction in 1910. Once good headlights were developed and cars could safely be taken out at night, they became much more useful.

In 1909, the Lamberts offered six models, from a $800 runabout to a $2,000 seven-passenger tonneau. Simplicity was featured in the promotional catalog with most copy going to the description of the friction drive transmission, "its reliability, ease of control and economy of maintenance." By 1910, the engines Lambert used were designed by the company and outsourced, so they were actually built by other companies: Buda, Continental, Davis, Rutenber and Treber. The production level for both 1906 and 1907 was 1,200 cars. 1910 was the peak year of production during which the Company had possibly 600 employees who produced 3,000 vehicles. In 1910, there were fewer than 200 automobiles owners in all of Anderson.

The top Lambert models were large cars of refinement and precision. They could easily seat five passengers on the leather upholstery. Four-cylinders provided a lot of power and could achieve up to 60 mph. The lowest models were 16 hp and cost $1,000. All models had two large gas lamps with a generator, two oil lamps and a 40" flexible tube horn. Honk! Honk!

Lambert car production was unique in that the entire vehicle was made within the factory. The Lamberts were manufacturers, not assemblers, as some brands were. Like their father before them, the brothers organized production to include all aspects of the automobile under one roof. The only exception was mentioned previously, that in some later models some Lambert-designed engines were made off-site. Thus with most components made in-house, John had dominion over all the different parts of all the vehicles, the engine, the transmission, the chassis and body. He meddled and tinkered continuously. All details of the workings of his machines received special attention and consequently, he came up with hundreds of new ideas for improvements. John innovated all aspects of the car. In turn he applied for patent protection for his ideas and got hundreds of patents. With six hundred patents to his name at the end of his life, one can imagine the scope and variety of things John got involved in. I have highlighted certain achievements and aspects, but the story goes beyond my descriptions of gasoline engines and "everything on springs". For example, the chain John developed for his drive mechanism was special, for it was silent. He came up with an innovative design that was very different from any previous chain. It looks like a woven belt one wears around one's waist made entirely of steel. The effect was to stifle noise.

Along with John's automobile-related patents are a variety of others; for example he patented a time clock in 1896 indicating his involvement in the mechanical aspects of employee behavior and plant management. Other brothers also entered the inventing game. Al, the moneyman, had patents for the three-ring binder and foldout sofa. Younger brothers had farm-related patents. Ray held patents related to tractor technology; my dad and my brother Stephen hold patents (or share a patent) related to lawn equipment, for a total of five generations of Lambert patent-holders, including John's father George: George, John, Ray, William and Stephen.

John's father modeled for his boys the importance of getting ideas patented. In order to defend against those who would steal his ideas, John did secure patent protection. From there he could defend his ideas in court if necessary by making a Federal case of it. There are two such cases I know of when he did just that. He sued and won them both. One was against the Carter Car Company of Detroit and the other was against the Waltham Manufacturing Company here in Massachusetts. This company manufactured the popular Orient Buckboard. Both companies were using John's friction drive transmission in their models and in both cases, the judge ordered them to pay a royalty to Lambert on each unit sold.

John worked on tractor technology. My understanding of my great-grandfather's pioneering automotive career leads me to suspect that his role in tractor history has yet to be told. His family had a primary interest in farm work for two generations; the pole and shaft market was still a mainstay for this family enterprise. The Lamberts came out with their first crawler tractor in 1904. These machines had tracks not wheels, a technology developed to counter the problem of tractor wheels getting stuck in soft mud. John was looking for the best way to move heavy loads without sinking into the field. Alongside automobile and truck production, the Lamberts developed several lines of tractors, a crawler field tractor and a steel-hoofed orchard model. Tractors were loaded and ready to ship to California when the Great Flood of 1913 hit. John took one of the tractors off the railroad car and set it up to run the Lambert engine at the Anderson *Bulletin*, so that the one-page paper could disseminate information to its desperate readership.

Business interest in citrus orchards entitled the family to travel to sunny locations. I saw pictures of them all in Florida and in California, even Minnie. Perhaps while on vacation (John's two youngest brothers lived in St. Petersburg) John witnessed orange growers in their orchards, for he set about designing a tractor to help in their specific tasks. He worked on an unusual wheel tread that had special retracting flaps that cleaned mud away as it turned. He placed the driver's seat low behind the tractor body, rather than high and on top, in order to avoid tree limbs. I have a child's model of the Lambert orchard tractor that was produced for promotional purposes. Manufacture of the orchard tractor began in 1912. Sales of this model accumulated in orange-growing regions, particularly California and Florida. Ray was eager to expand this part of the business and saw vast California as the place where the orange industry would flourish. Shipments of tractors to California were a sizable part of the Anderson output. A letter dated 1913 tells of a Lambert Orchard Tractor winning the Gold Rank Medal at the Third Annual Orange Show in San Bernardiao, California and of beating all others in a weight pulling contest the next day. A testimonial letter from the Mayor, along with three Councilmen of the City of San Bernardino, makes explicit this demonstration. Testimonials claimed the Lambert steel-hoofed tractor could pull equal to a six-horse team, only faster. I saw another letter that put John in Miami, Florida in 1918. He was setting up tractor sales. A 1914 letter referred to John's trip to Wisconsin to rectify a problem with a Lambert tractor.

With the big initial success in California, Ray went to work to put a deal together for an El Seguno, California manufacturing facility. A front page headline story (August 13, 1914) in the El Segundo paper told of the plans for a new 12,000 square foot brick factory building on a six acre site to be completed in time for several carloads of machinery to be installed, having arrived carefully timed "from the east" by train. They predicted "the plant will be turning out tractors within ninety days." The article claimed Lambert tractors were sold all over the country and "in many foreign countries." Ray was trying to orchestrate a strong start, and with plans to employ 100 men, convincing their new neighbors of their success was important. John spent a lot of time in El Segundo, California helping with the plans. He also continued to develop his designs. He may have met Benjamin Holt, but certainly heard of him, for Holt was headquartered in Oregon and the two men both hold patents for the continuous wheel tread. This technology was the inspiration for military tanks. Ray moved his family out to the West Coast (my father was born in California). Through economic bad luck or other means, the venture did not work out. In a letter John Lee writes about the cause of the demise. One of their primary investors, a Mr. S. J. Smith, died suddenly and his heirs withdrew their support. Mr. Smith was the Lambert distributing agent in Los Angeles selling their Indiana-made tractors in California, Arizona and Nevada. After the project was abandoned, Ray went to work for Howard Hughes's father at Hughes Tool Company selling oil well drilling equipment before moving back to the Midwest. John moved back to Anderson where Minnie kept the homestead and continued to invent better ways for doing what he saw before him.

There was tragedy on the factory floor. On Christmas day, 1905, John's forty-two year old brother-in-law John Luvici who worked at the factory died. He had been a civil engineer, but when he developed poor eyesight he took a job running a steam engine on the factory floor. He reportedly had blood poisoning, whatever that meant, and died after a long illness. His untimely death was felt by all. Every employee signed a card for the widow, Minnie's sister Dora, who with her children became part of John's household at 705 Hendricks Street. Dora sewed muslin covers for Lambert cars. An envelope was passed through the plant so that each employee could add a few cents to the fund for the widow and her three children. I have the list of names and a printed picture of the plant members.

Dora was by all family accounts spirited. By the same accounts Minnie never smiled. I wonder if Dora ever got her married older sister to crack her dour Victorian expression. One Saturday night after going out in her Lambert car, Dora returned being escorted by the Town Marshall. He told her family, "It is a wonderful machine, but she might kill somebody." He must have found the car's acetylene lamps she was using for finding her way in the dark insufficient. Years after her husband's death, Dora married President Warren G.Harding's father sometime during the son's scandal-filled Presidency, 1921-23. He was a doctor, like their father old Dr. Kelley who had died so long ago. The elder Harding must have expected a certain standard of decorum from his young wife that he did not apply to himself. Several marital indiscretions of his came to light and she quietly divorced him after four years. As a descendent of hers said, "He had a zipper problem." I remember my grandmother, Ray's wife, told a story of being at a garden party where the Hardings were and how "pushy" the future President's wife was. Many, including she, believed he rode to the White House on his wife's ambition. My grandmother told me, "He never would have been President. It was her idea." Just as some calamitous scandals were about to break in the news, Warren Harding died while on a trip to California with his wife.

After Dora's divorce she lived between Anderson and Union City, for it was in Union City she developed breast cancer which was successfully treated (I'm quoting an old relative) "by the doctor pouring poison directly onto the site". I love my colorful "Dorrie stories". She lived with her daughter Miriam who was an expert weaver. Their household was busy and a center for visitors, for many were attracted to their lively and interesting talk. Dora died in 1939. Dora's daughter Miriam Luvici was a great source of Lambert information as in her later years she became friends with Dan and Barb Davis in Anderson, who befriended me and told stories that they had heard from "Aunt Miriam." As natives of Anderson, Dan and Barb had the opportunity to know many witnesses; for example, Dan's grandfather who started as a horse trader, later became an auto mechanic. He had stories of working on Lambert vehicles. Dan was puzzled by another tale from the man who sold John his cigars: John always wanted to buy the cigar buried deepest in the case. Hmmm. I think he considered that particular cigar's moisture to be the best preserved.

With the outbreak of World War One the Lamberts cooperated with the government and under contract with the War Department turned their operations and all their manufacturing capabilities over to the war effort. Military fire engines, artillery shells and caisson wheels were made in the Lambert factory in Anderson. One source reported that using Howe-designed bodies, Lambert and Ford joined forces to produce one hundred fire trucks for the War Department. The Howe Fire Engine Company, established in 1872 making horse-drawn fire fighting wagons, had long been a partner with Lambert. As war broke out Mae recalled that the factory became "off limits to all visitors" to follow the security rules imposed by the War Department.

The technology John developed for steel-hoofed tractors was easily converted to military application, making "moving gun trucks" or *tanks* a great technological achievement at just the right time. I suspect he may have been personally involved in the development of the era's new war machine, the tank. Journalists were calling for an armored petrol tractor to defend against machine-guns. The first tank prototype was British; "Little Willie" came out in 1915. Tanks tipped the balance of weaponry to the Allied side. John and Benjamin Holt, also a manufacturer of agricultural equipment, independently both worked on the innovations that were dubbed the "caterpillar" tread. This referred to the continuously revolving tractor feet, a design to facilitate movement over uneven ground. He was thinking of moving citrus fruit through a muddy field, but he in fact also gave direct help to winning the war!

By 1915 automobile sales started to drop. Lambert slashed their prices but the tide was going out. In an economy move, the next year John came out with a 6-cylinder chassis to be used both for a large luxury model automobile and for his trucks.

John had watched the revolutionary success of Ford's ideas of mass production spread over the marketplace and knew his own career had been placed at a crossroads. Once the war was over, John could see Big Change was in order. In order to compete with Ford's dominance, John understood that he would have to expand on a mammoth scale, but he was not willing to do that. Henry Ford was putting out three hundred cars a day while John's facilities were set up for three. John decided it was time to re-organize. He would bow out of the automobile business in order to focus on the rest of the Lambert line. In his last year of production he sold fifty automobiles, all large six-cylinder, four-door tourers. In 1917, the car models were dropped, leaving trucks, tractors and gasoline engines. The following year, trucks were also dropped.

But until that happened, the Car Years provided a glamorous, picturesque, happy time. Within a community of like-minded men, John and the early car pioneers visualized together a future unimagined by most Americans and set into motion an industry that put America behind the wheel of a gasoline-powered automobile.

Chapter 10

Later, the Yard Rake

The side yard of the home on 705 Hendricks Street as it looks today is void of the large shed that was constructed as a storage barn with workspace for John. The original wooden structure next to the wide driveway was built with the house in 1899. From the days he first had his factory built in Anderson, John Lambert did a lot of walking. He walked to work at his plant a few blocks away and when he needed further travel, he walked to a livery barn to pick up a horse and carriage. There were at least two liveries within a two-block radius of his home. The shed in the driveway probably held a wagon or a carriage or their pieces, the household's tools to care for the outside and probably a variety of things not immediately identifiable, pieces of tools and machines of worth only to John. But the old style transportation fittings were surely abandoned within just a few years as Mae's gasoline-powered car took over the driveway and enough room inside the shed to keep the new auto paraphernalia protected from Indiana weather. Harnesses and bridles gave way to pneumatic tubes and wrenches. Mae's automobile was likely stored off-site of their home at an "auto hotel" such as the one run by her Uncle Harry. Hers was the prototype and so a harbinger of many Lambert cars to be parked in this area beside the house. Throughout the years of Lambert car production this part of Minnie's domain saw beautiful machines. There would have been specimens of the most elaborate cars of the era parked as though poised at various angles and out in front of the house by the concrete curb in which the impression of John's signature is still clear. The first two decades of the twentieth century featured large 4 and 6 cylinder, 30 horsepower, five passenger tonneaus, a colorful assortment like bright royal blue with yellow striping, luxurious leather clad models, with shiny brass lanterns.

On a Sunday afternoon a variety of automobiles might be parked while guests lingered inside, no doubt the newest and most sophisticated cars the car makers could show to each other. I would think John and his automotive friends, executives and mechanics alike, puffing on cigars and discussing what they saw, would have genuine interests in driving each other's machines. Perhaps it never happened or perhaps test-driving was a regular part of the recreational activities on tree-lined Hendricks. It was a beautiful setting for commercial pictures as well. Some Lambert promotional photos were taken in this neighborhood. My favorite photos of John's cars were posed on the expansive grounds of the Anderson Country Club. When John was out of the business, the driveway was nonetheless decorated with beautiful cars, a few of which were gifts from friends still in the business. At two points my great-grandfather drove a Haynes, maybe gifts from his good friend Elwood; John also owned an Apperson. Perhaps John owned both in order to compare the work of the two feuding automobile makers from up the road in Kokomo. Perhaps their gifts were tokens of appreciation for his silence on the priority matter. The debate of the two Kokomo competing claims had flared up in the media during this time.

Long after the production of Lambert cars ceased and throughout the 1920's, John and Minnie continued to entertain their friends in the automobile world. Mae remembers the "Dodge boys conferring with my father and swapping stories." They no doubt debated the deals other car makers were involved in and the court cases that forced them to take sides. Henry Ford and his wife were guests just once at John and Minnie's table. I think that visit was the origin of a certain legendary comment by Ray. My dad quoted his dad as saying he did not like the way Ford spoke to his wife. Here is the likely setting to have witnessed such marital interaction. Hopefully at the more congenial gatherings the automakers philosophized over the directions the business of selling cars moved around in and the effect it had on people. Perhaps the parties dimmed after the death of Elwood Haynes in 1925. John was to live for twenty-seven more years.

As John's retirement progressed, the cavernous wooden shed by the driveway acquired the accoutrements of an accomplished inventor. For a while in more recent times, a grandnephew lived in the shed. How I wish to go back in time and visit that shed, to gaze upon the tools kept and used, the projects in process or stashed away. Aunt Jean told me the walls were covered with tools hung on nails. Also, John had two Lincoln-Douglas Debate posters up on the wall that had belonged to his parents. I am proud to claim my ancestors as Lincoln Republicans, anti-slavery all the way. Other treasures from John's shed are lost. We can look at the workshop re-creations of inventors contemporary to John and surmise what he might have surrounded himself with, but we can't know for sure what this unique and prolific man had about him. The laboratory of Thomas Edison is on display at the Henry Ford Museum. Edison had over 1200 patents, an average of one every two weeks. John accumulated 600, one on average every four weeks. John's shed became a den of invention, a focus of curiosity to neighborhood children and lore to their parents. Reports confirm he had an "oven" or kiln for heating steel, a lathe and a wall of tools.

Equally happy, if less glamorous, is one of my dad's central memories of his grandfather: playing checkers with him outside of the big house in the driveway. They had set up a card table while the two of them were sitting on folding chairs. There is no doubt my dad loved the old car maker with the adoration of a grandson and John was up to the task of maintaining his good impression on the young boy. Young Billy did not have daily opportunities to spend time with his extended family because Dayton was a long ride away but their frequent visits bred closeness nonetheless. Dad recalls his grandfather's affability, his patience and humor as he challenged and encouraged his young foe at the board. Dad denies the genius inventor let him win and forgets who did.

The driveway was also the location of the infamous "yard broom caper" wherein this affable old man almost led my innocent father and numerous other young people into a life of crime! The story starts with another of John's Big Hits. Faced each autumn with a yard full of fallen leaves, John devised his own version of the best tool to meet that challenge. In the old wooden shed he designed and made what we now call a rake, a metal version of the "yard broom". He received his patent in 1937. He was seventy-seven years old. He set up production in a building in downtown Anderson, where the pieces were made and assembled. It was simple, repetitive work, tempering and cutting the steel into strips, lining up and attaching the thin metal strips into a crossbow-device by punching each one into its slot and thus making the row lie securely flat. The last adjustment was to snap the headdress-like design into place at the end of a long wooden handle. John's rake manufacturing career lasted for several years at which point he sold the patent rights to the manufacturing giant American Hoe and Shovel out of Toledo. John then changed his original design somewhat and continued to assemble rakes out of the shed by the driveway. He recruited his grandchildren and the neighborhood kids to help and then gave away what they made.

Mae must have known what was going on and became witness to the crimes in the driveway. When one of the rakes passed to someone's hands from American Hoe, a lawyer showed up right there at the house to close down the domestic "manufacturing source". Mae stood with her eighty-year-old father who was ordered by a judge to cease his production of rakes. I don't think John or his daughter thought much of the boys from American Hoe.

After the demise of the California dreams, Ray returned to the Midwest and settled in Dayton, Ohio with his young family where he set up a soap dispenser business. The Depression years beat more than one of Ray's schemes. My dad remembers the up and down progress of his dad's endeavors until Ray returned to the ol' family standby. He bought land near Ansonia and built a beautiful redbrick factory. Lambert, Inc. manufactured garden tools and lawn mowers. My dad continued to build Ray's business after his father's early death and successfully manufactured lawn and industrial floor sweepers that put me through college. I'm ever grateful to them all. I was raised in the same Dayton, Ohio community in which my dad grew up among many descendants of inventive, industrial revolutionists.

The time John spent commuting to California was always considered temporary, as Minnie stayed in Anderson. The Buckeye Manufacturing Company went into receivership Nov. 9, 1921 so it no longer existed. For thirty years the Lambert family successfully rode the waves of the marketplace with this company. In 1924 John had left California for good to return to 705 Hendricks Street. The slate was clean but there were new endeavors to pursue and new ideas to explore.

The Lambert family enterprises acquired a whimsical side with the arrival of grandchildren. In the 1920's the Lamberts designed a line of toys; whether they saw manufacture or what happened to the prototypes I don't know. I think we can assume that it was John who designed the toys for his grandchildren. My dad's older sister Patty and their older cousin John were toddler models for the promotional pictures. There is a photo album of the 8×10 pictures in the Lee collection that shows a Lambert-made sled, scooter, dolly, ice skates, a wagon, tricycle, hobbyhorse and an airplane to sit in and "ride". In a combination rocking-horse-kiddie car the forward motion of the rocker sent the vehicle ahead a foot or more and thus the child could seesaw across the parlor floor. This little toy has John's signatures all over it, a simple mechanical concept doing a big and clever job.

During those years John patented a lock for the steering wheel and entered a deal with Ford who used the design on their models. My Dad remembers his grandfather's talking about a scheme to buy old telephone poles and turn them into toothpicks. Even with failing eyesight, this devoted husband invented a kitchen convenience for his wife. After eating a pancake breakfast he walked across the driveway to his shed and emerged in the late afternoon with his design for her, a trigger-operated pancake flipper. As he lost his hearing Ray tried to supply his father with a hearing aid and bought an expensive piece. John was not a compliant patient; his curiosity overcame his use of it and rather than wear it he took it apart. To aid his failing eyesight he designed a large magnifying glass inside a circle of light, on a stand. As the house was renovated he designed a brace to fasten down wood flooring. The floor brace patent was issued in 1942; John was eighty-two. He was observing what was going on around him and he was still itchy to make it better.

John lost the bulk of his fortune in 1929 due to a bank failure. The day before the failure, John had decided to withdraw his money in order to place it in more secure accounts and set out on foot down the block to the bank. The bank owner, a neighbor and a man John had considered a friend, implored him not to withdraw by claiming his action would create panic among his other customers. John walked home without his money and the owner closed his bank that night. John lost about a million dollars (another story said $200,000). John was not the only Andersonian to lose all to this unpopular fellow. Minnie, being more socially conscious and competitive than her husband, voiced the frustration for the couple. John never referred to the incident and was never bitter over the loss. Money is not what motivated him. Minnie said there were times after that it was only the dividend payments from her stocks in the Pioneer Pole and Shaft Company that kept her and John afloat.

After the death of her husband Claude Lee in 1939, Mae moved back into the Hendricks Street home to help keep an eye on her aging parents. She broke the big home up into apartments and collected rents to supplement her salary as a clerk in a jewelry store. Hers was the steady income that put food on the table. Minnie died in 1949 and John died in 1952. I was born in 1950.

My dad loved his two antique Lambert cars with glee. His first acquisition was the 1910 four seater (six if four in the back are kids). Found in Minnesota in excellent condition, this 4 –cylinder, 35 horse power model was sold in 1910 for $1,200. Originally black, my Dad had it painted yellow. It has a Davis engine made to Lambert specifications. The second acquisition was an earlier model. My dad bought a bright red, two-cylinder two-seat runabout made in 1908. Both are in running condition and participate in the Ohio City parades.

Meanwhile in 1952 in upstate New York at Grand Island, a man named John J. Lambert came upon a pile of iron bones inside an abandoned ice house. When Jack, as he was called, first stood before the pile of rusting metal, had he known of the early auto pioneer named John W. Lambert? When he lifted the rotting wooden panel from an old door to reveal the pieces of a deconstructed old car, did he know this car bore his name? If not, he soon learned and developed glee as well. Collecting the pile of junk onto a flatbed truck he began his work of re-making every piece and putting together his 1909 Lambert automobile. Jack figured out the right way and built a prize-winning car. For one problem he found a specialist who flew in from the West Coast just to work on the car. When new wooden wheels were needed, Jack started an antique wheel business to supply the needs for himself and other old car lovers. He or a specialist re-made by hand each of the parts, big and small, mechanical and structural, including the fenders and body panels. This car received countless awards including a five-foot high Best in Show trophy at the 1959 National Convention of the AACA.

It must have been true love for this Mr. Lambert. Jack took his car to shows and competitions and re-enactments of famous car races including the 1959 Glidden tour. He drove the Buffalo to Detroit route across Canada on the 100th Anniversary of the Henry Ford Museum and landed on the front page of the Detroit *Free Press*. In fact this automobile received a lot of publicity including write-ups in *AutoWeek* and *Automobile Quarterly*. The stimulus for Scott Bailey to investigate the case for Lambert priority, Jack's car was a beautiful specimen. Being red made it stand out. He took it all over the South and Midwest. When he wasn't out in Utah or Ohio he had it in local parades in Buffalo or took it to Rochester for the car shows. Jack visited old Lambert family sites, although he was only related through love of the car. Often he took his son Scott on these adventures who remembers the rugged ride of the open vehicle and the numerous stops to fix a tire or something else. Jack of course carried his own tools and made his own repairs. Scott remembers a run out of Bar Harbor, Maine he took as a boy with his father in the 1909 Lambert along with twenty to thirty other brass-era entrants. They traveled a two-lane road with no shoulders. Breakdowns were tough to repair, some necessitating the vehicle being trailered to a machine shop. The purpose of this adventure was to re-enact the old conditions. Stealing my thoughts Scott said it was not that much fun. I think we take our AC and high suspension rides for granted.

At times Jack was accompanied by his wife Marshia who sheltered herself by wearing a duster, a long coat popular with riders in the early times for protecting one's clothes from the upturned dirt of the road and endured bugs in the face, also a feature of the ride, before wrapping her head in netting and a hat as ladies did when the car was new. Marshia told me that when the car would break down as it usually did, a crowd would form to share with Jack the marvel of the old machine. She told me her basement Rec

Room is filled with loving cups and awards that her husband collected with his old Lambert car.

Jack climbed Pike's Peak in this car! My mother took us kids on that ride in a 1965 Bonneville station wagon, a two ton vehicle that had "wide track stability with 90 cubic feet of cargo space" and, hello, power steering. The car was awarded a bumper sticker to claim it. I can only imagine what it would be like in a 1909 2-cylinder open-air roadster with 20 HP. Jack said the climb was easy but the trip down was hair-raising. He knew the brakes could easily have cut out but they did not. Jack's Lambert did the job; it climbed Pike's Peak and brought itself with Jack safely back down.

At a car meet in Indiana with his 1909 Lambert, Jack met Dan and Barb Davis and told them about another pile of pieces of Lambert car back in upstate New York. This is how Dan came to own his Lambert. The pieces turned out to be a 1912 torpedo 4-cylinder Lambert automobile that is now at the Indianapolis Museum.

I spoke with another Lambert who had glee in his voice when I asked about his Lambert cars. Terry Lambert, also not a blood relative of mine, lives in Nebraska and owns not one, not two, but six Lambert cars. He told his tale of waiting thirty-two years for one of them in a 1993 article in *Horseless Gazette*. He first heard of the car in 1953. In 1955 he made an offer but the owner did not want to sell and put it in storage. Terry kept in touch. With only 186 miles on it, it was a prize worth waiting for. Thirty-two years later, in 1987 he got his call to come and get it. The acquisition story of another of Terry's Lamberts bears repeating. Because Terry was always looking for One More, he wore a T-shirt at car shows that read "Wanted: Lambert Cars and Parts". Someone came forward to report a 1908 Model M 4-cylinder Lambert with rare shaft-drive and an oval radiator. What a find! There were pictures in the magazine and yes, the familiar Lambert logo was on that oval honeycomb radiator front. Beautiful!

Discoveries are very exciting. In 1972 the remains of a 1913 Lambert Model 99 with its friction disks were discovered in Sterling, Illinois. The man who found it said, "This must have been a tremendously large car as everything is so heavy and well-put together."

In 2001 a Lambert family friend donated a beautiful two-cylinder, 20 horse power 1909 Lambert roadster to the Carillon Historical Park in Dayton, Ohio. A snappy white car with red leather seats, it is very close in appearance to the original four-wheeled prototype John built for his daughter Mae perhaps ten years previous. The Carillon car even has a rumble seat. Best of all it is on permanent display among other antique cars and available for the public to view. This park along the Great Miami River was close enough to my home growing up to hear the chiming bells. Its twenty-five historic buildings hold hundreds of artifacts, including the Wright Brothers' airplane, an 1835 B&O steam locomotive and remnants of the Miami-Erie Canal.

In 1965 the citizens of Ohio City, Ohio organized the first annual Lambert Day Festival. This celebration included the automaker's daughter Mae Lambert Lee who was almost eighty. Also at the event was retired druggist James Swoveland who testified to seeing and riding in John's 1891 prototype. My dad was there with my brothers and his mother, Ray's widow, all from Dayton and John Lee brought his family from Anderson. Under the leadership of Emilie and Mayor Wert the festival has now been expanded to three days of community activities including a big parade of classic automobiles and farm equipment, school kids and local businesses along the same streets John entertained earlier citizens with his three-wheeled wonder. I have been there for the event in recent years and thoroughly enjoyed their company and soaking up the ambiance of the cornfields and gently rolling hills of the Ohio countryside. They had ballgames and carnival rides, cookouts and displays of historic photos and military artifacts. The photos show Ohio City in blizzards, tornadoes, flood and fire as well as pictures of old cars and engines. There is a beautiful wall mural inside one of their community buildings by William G. Book of Van Wert, Ohio that shows John Lambert driving his famous three-wheeled automobile. Museum plans are in the works including making Ohio City a National Historic Site. I would like to see a rendering of my great grandfather's Ohio City prototype, the little three-wheeled wonder, placed in the seal of the Great State of Ohio, just as the Wright Brothers' plane has, most appropriately, recently been added.

In 1976 Anderson, Indiana held a huge Bicentennial Parade that included fifty-three floats, ten bands, a live lion, one hundred fifty horses and my dad's two cars. He drove one; John Lee drove the other. The next year two Historical Markers were dedicated, one at 705 Hendricks Street which says:

Lambert House, Built 1899

Home of John W. Lambert, inventor and builder of America's first successful gasoline-powered automobile in 1891. With more than 600 patents credited in his lifetime, this pioneer is accorded the title "Father of the Gearless Transmission" for a unique friction drive applied to Lambert cars and trucks produced in Anderson beginning 1905.

The other marker was placed at the site of Buckeye Manufacturing Company, 1803 Columbus Ave in downtown Anderson, but it is gone now. The building burned in 1980's.

Lambert promotional material for these early cars has survived to the current day. The official yearly catalogs were well-designed with beautiful photographs and have extensive descriptions of the merchandise and manufacturing process. Other booklets also contain letters from customers. My ancestors were very interested in feedback, quick to fix any problems which they knew would squash negative chatter and not shy about soliciting compliments. One testimonial to the superior quality of the Lambert automobiles was from Lambert owner and baseball legend Hans "Honas" Wagner, known as the Flying Dutchman. A baseball superstar of the first decade of the Twentieth Century, Hans hit a .329 career average. He was one of five inducted in the first group to enter the Baseball Hall of Fame. A shortstop for the Pittsburgh Pirates, Hans Wagner played in fifteen World Series games, including the 1909 World Series against Ty Cobb's Detroit Tigers. In that series, Hans stole six bases to Cobb's two; to add injury to that insult, he picked off Cobb at second, leaving a cut on his mouth that needed three stitches. Hans Wagner was a league leader in hitting (eight years), RBI's (two years) and steals (five years) and the first player to have his signature on a Louisville slugger (1905). A long-limbed boxy man, he was also bowlegged. Jeered as "octopus" by the crowd and called "krauthead" by opposing players, his 1909 baseball card is now the most expensive in baseball, worth 1.62 million dollars. In a crowd-pleasing burst of showmanship, he would scoop dirt up with the ball in a play so that dust followed his throw like a comet. Hans Wagner had an exceptional eye and back in his home state among the up and down topography of Pennsylvania, he saw the car that best took the hills; it was a Lambert. He knew speed and he knew strength and he choose to drive a 1907 Model H Lambert car. In his testimonial he calls his Lambert "a wonder." Well, Hans, so were you. He writes:

Gentlemen: Your Model H car which I received in August certainly is all you claim for it, and as a hill climber is a wonder, as you know I do most of my motoring here among the hills, and there is none too steep for my car, with the 4-cylinder Rutenber motor shaft drive, which is almost noiseless (sic). There are two cars in this vicinity of your manufacture which found the going easy for them, and as I was looking for a car for these hills, your car appealed to me; and as to speed, I have found mine just as you represented it, and am well pleased with my purchase.

Yours respectfully,
John Hans Wagner,
Pittsburg (sic) Base Ball Club Carnegie, Pa.

Dan Davis, Anderson native and Lambert collector and historian, gave talks on my great-grandfather complete with slides. He spoke before groups in Anderson and throughout the Midwest. His widow was gracious enough to share Dan's material with me.

From an unfinished book, Dan writes:

> That John Lambert's name belongs with the genius of his time is irrefutable. John built and operated the first gasoline powered vehicle in America, was a pioneer in the design of gas and gasoline powered stationary engines, tractors, crawler tractors, automobiles, trucks and street cars. He patented the Gearless Friction Drive transmission, was involved in the construction of at least one airplane and held over 600 patents on an amazing amount of hardware, including a barn beam auger and his final major product, a better yard rake. He was truly a giant and a man of vision, who always understood what was happening around him.

The following words were spoken by Dan at an Ohio City Lambert Day Festival. I am presumptuous enough to end with Dan's ending. His words:

> That we come together once a year to celebrate the life and times of John William Lambert, I believe, is a fine thing. JW and some of his peers were truly giants that walked among us. They paved the way for what has become for the vast majority of us a good and decent way of life free from the drudgery and isolation that had plagued other generations before us. This technology for the masses was the legacy they imparted to our civilization. They quite literally changed the world. When the door of the machinery store was flung open and the little three-wheeler bucked and popped and lurched for the first time in the sunlight on Carmean Street, I wonder if any of the amazed onlookers had an inkling that they had witnessed history. With wood and iron, leather and horsehair, grease and gasoline, and a bit of electricity, John had drawn back the curtain and had shown the citizenry a brief glimpse into the future. The world would never be the same! He was a giant that walked in Ohio City...I hope we never run out of giants

A Gallery of Images

The Walter Lewis Photo of America's Original Car. This rare photo shows the three-wheeled buggy JWL operated on the streets of Ohio City, Ohio in 1891. It had a single cylinder, 4 cycle motor and reached 15 mph. It weighed 560 pounds and was offered for sale for $550.00

John William Lambert, 1860-1952, Inventor of America's First Gasoline Automobile. Known in his day as the Father of the Gradual Transmission, Lambert held over 600 patents most of which relate to the automobile industry and is perhaps the most significant over-looked American inventor

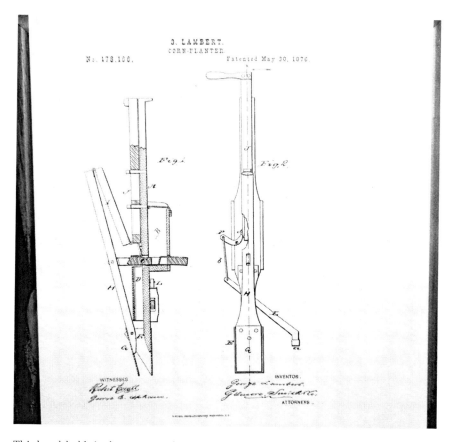

This hand-held single-row corn planter was John's first patent. The invention revolutionized corn planting at the time and sold nationally. The farm boy was 16.

"He made his daughter a car!" and then John used it to collect orders as he founded the Union Automobile Company in 1902. Note the rumble seat. JWL manufactured automobiles, trucks and tractors until the First World War when he joined with Henry Ford to produce fire trucks for the War Department.

The Buckeye. Here is one of America's first gasoline engines, a Lambert Buckeye (factory #5378) with its owner, historian Dan Davis. Although John's original automobile prototype did not sell, John manufactured his engine and sold them like hotcakes.

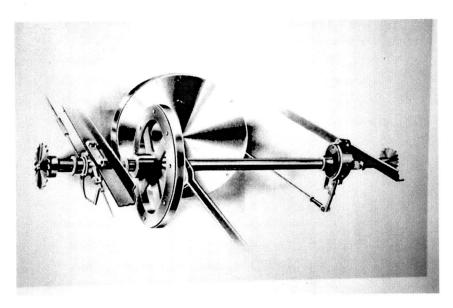

Gearless Friction Drive. The two perpendicular disks of John's transmission offered an entirely smooth start and acceleration. In extensive road tests his transmission beat the standard type every time and is a technology still in use today.

The Factory Floor. The Lambert Automobile Manufacturing Company was in Anderson, Indiana and at its peak was a top American seller, producing 3,000 cars and trucks a year. Here is a floor full of installed disk transmissions. Note the large windows, important for light.

LAMBERT MODEL H
PRICE $2000

This luxury Lambert Model H of 1907 was the automobile personally chosen by legendary Hans "Honas" Wagner, Baseball Hall of Famer. Hans had an exceptional eye and back in his home among the hills of Pennsylvania he saw the car that best took those hills. He knew strength and speed and he choose to drive a Lambert.

John liked to test the cars himself and drove his vehicles up this harrowing wooden testing ramp across from his factory in Anderson, Indiana. Men on the structure demonstrate the scale of this challenge.

Carol Jean Lambert

The look of a winner. Demonstrating endurance and speed, road races were devised to convince the public to give up their horses. Here is John and fans after a Chicago race.

CPSIA information can be obtained at www.ICGtesting.com
Printed in the USA
BVOW04s1652060514

352728BV00002B/4/P

9 781939 166319